FUTUWWAH

Futuwwah and Raising Males into Sacred Manhood

Author: Dawud Walid
Proofreading: Wordsmith
Design & Typesetting: www.igpconsultants.com | info@igpconsultants.com

Paperback: 978-1-952306-38-9
International Mass Print: 978-1-952306-39-6

Proudly printed in the USA and United Kingdom.

info@imamghazalipublishing.com | www.imamghazalipublishing.com

Distribution by Sattaur Publishing Group
www.sattaurpublishing.com | info@sattaurpublishing.com

FUTUWWAH

AND RAISING MALES INTO SACRED MANHOOD

AUTHORED BY

Dawud Walid

FOREWORD BY

Maulana Asim Ayub

CONTENTS

FOREWORD 7
AUTHOR'S PREFACE 17
INTRODUCTION 21

What is Futuwwah? 29
Truthfulness 39
Loving and Loathing for the Sake of Allah 47
Vigilant Care 57
Humility 63
Service Towards Others 69
Good Conduct Towards Parents 73
Deference Towards Scholars and Spiritual Mentors 79
Generosity 85
Modesty 89
Restraining Sexual Desires 93
Courage 101
Sincere Advice 107
Brotherhood 113
Pardoning 125
Honouring Neighbours and Guests 129
Honourable Altruism 135

CONCLUSION 141
NOTES 147
BIBLIOGRAPHY 161

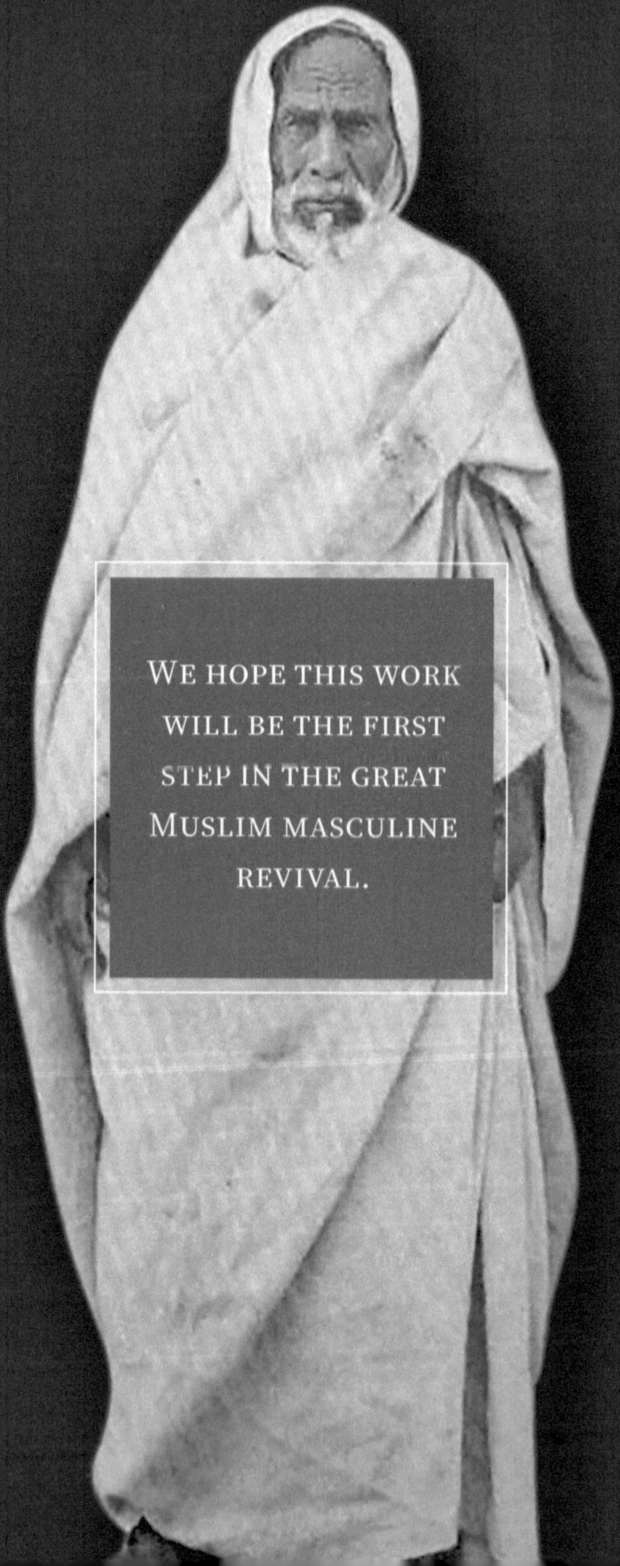

We hope this work will be the first step in the great Muslim masculine revival.

Foreword

The early Muslims were renowned for their immense perseverance and steadfastness in the path of Islam, going through colossal amounts of hardship in Makkah and Madinah that produced paragons of faith who would carry forth the religion of Islam after the death of the Chosen One ﷺ. Among them was the early companion, ʿUtbah ibn Ghazwān, one of the foremost military commanders in the Caliphate's wars against Sassanid Persia. In a narration from the Shamāʾil Muḥammadiyyah of Imam al-Tirmidhī, he reminisces about those early days of Muslim struggle that made him the man he became. Standing upon the pulpit, he preaches to his men:

> I was the seventh of seven people [to accept Islam] with the Messenger of Allah. We had no food except for the leaves of trees that caused sores to develop around our mouths. I discovered a mantle and took it, splitting it between myself and Saʿd ibn Mālik. There is none from the seven of us except that he is now the leader of a city – and you will experience first-hand the rulers after us![1]

This powerful throwback to harder times shows the appreciation the early Muslims had for the blessing of hardship and its preparatory role in nurturing strong and steadfast leaders. It functioned primarily as a form of primarily, spiritual, but also physical initiation that produced a calibre of men upon which this tremendous faith could so securely depend. Now, standing at the frontiers of the Muslim lands, outnumbered by Persian forces, our Master ʿUtbah makes it very clear why he is the man that Allah and his Caliph have chosen for this momentous feat.

ʿUtbah closes his sermon with a stark warning, making clear that the Muslims should treasure the rulership of these prophetically initiated men, men who would enter His presence as seekers and leave as beacons of guidance for those still lost in the dark. Yet, as they would slowly leave this earthly domain, their positions would be filled by egotistical tyrants whose materialistic greed would spell despair for those unfortunate enough to live under their oppressive rule. It may be argued that we are experiencing a recurrence of those rulers today, a specific symptom of the terminal decline of masculinity and the loss of initiation in the modern age.

The idea that the male must go through some sort of 'rite of passage' is not a new, nor uniquely Islamic, phenomenon. Initiation is a process that transforms young impulsive boys into sturdy dependable men, and is ubiquitous in societies throughout human history.[2] What form that initiation took would vary depending on the culture it was embedded in, and the Islamic world was no exception. Islam's unique quality of taking from the goodness of its surroundings and discarding anything disagreeable to its ethical, moral, and theological framework meant it developed its own uniquely indigenous form of masculine initiation.[3] Pre-Islamic Arabian poetry is replete with references to the *fatā* – chivalric young man. In the pre-Islamic environment of a chaotic and fragile Bedouin existence, masculine strength and warriorship were strongly applauded – a sentiment readily co-opted by the early Muslims. The Chosen One states in an authentic narration that:

> The strong believer is better and more beloved to Allah than the weak believer, while there is [still] goodness in both.[4]

The great commentator of Hadith, Imam al-Nawawī explains this strength as one that manifests in having steadfast patience 'in the harms faced in the path of Allah.' With the descent of revelation, the pre-Islamic chivalrous young man had now been provided with a spiritual anchor.[5]

Futuwwah as an Institution

The Islamic institution of *futuwwah* (masculine chivalry) took great inspiration from pre-existing Persian and Turkic traditions of masculine initiation. The flood of new converts, and Islam's strong tradition of cultural appreciation, ensured that an indigenously Islamic ethos of masculine initiation, rooted in the developing science of *taṣawwuf*, made its appearance by the 5th Islamic century.[6] Finding its primary Islamic exemplar in the youthful devotedness of Imam ʿAlī, it always recognised that the greatest *Fityān* were those referenced in the Qur'an. From our Master Ibrāhīm destroying the idols of his people, the young men of the cave escaping the hedonistic polytheism of their society, the young man of the chapter of Burūj sacrificing his life for the sake of Allah, to Sayyidah Maryam's strength of faith in the face of societal opposition, the Qur'an is replete with examples of young men – and at times women – developing themselves as God-fearing slaves in the furnace of hardship. This all goes without mentioning the Chosen One himself – always lauded as the ultimate fountain of masculine chivalric strength.[7]

From these Qur'anic seeds sprouted transformative literature stretching throughout Islamic history: from the early writings of Imam al-Sulamī to the erudite Ḥanbalī theologian Ibn al-Qayyim, Futuwwah was seen as an indispensable rung in the ladder of Islamic spiritual development.[8] The definition of Imam Ḥārith al-Muḥāsibī, the great early spiritual sage, stands out for its Prophetic ethos: 'To be just, but to never seek justice.'[9]

At this stage, the demarcation of the *fatā* was complete; a strong, honest, generous man (or woman), independently assured in their faith, and a support for those struggling around him. A body of literature around *futuwwah* did not function alone, as Islam's communal and societal focus meant that these teachings were institutionalised into the 'Sufi' lodges and guilds, providing spiritual nourishment to young men in urban Muslim centres. Spiritual training was not their only forte, as *futuwwah* branched out into military fortress guilds at the borders of Muslim lands and even to occupational guilds that trained young men in manufacturing crafts whilst catering to their spiritual needs.[10] At times they simply functioned as informal caravansaries, taking care of travellers and people in poverty. It was after experiencing the immense generosity of one of these premodern 'food banks' that the famed traveller Ibn Battuta said, 'No people are more courteous to strangers, more readily supply them with food and other necessaries, or are more opposed to oppressors than they are.'[11]

Composed of predominantly unmarried men, these associations provided much needed social and economic welfare in an area filled with chaos amidst the debris of the collapsed Seljuk State. They were civic surrogates due to the lack of public institutions, ensuring that many young men in the area would not be sucked into the life of immoral self-destruction that was so pervasive at the time. The guilds and Sufi *futuwwah* lodges also laid the strong foundation for many a political revival, with the Sufi lodge of Imam ʿAbd al-Qādir al-Jīlānī credited for the later conquest of Jerusalem at the hands of Salaḥ al-dīn al-Ayyūbī.[12] The Sufi warrior – a spiritually mature being more in control of himself than any opponent – can be seen in the early Muslims through the likes of Imam ʿAbdullāh ibn al-Mubārak all the way to the modern anti-colonial Sufi sage, Hafiz ʿUmar Mukhtār.[13] The spiritual systems of masculine initiation functioned to equip the Ummah with a strong masculine backbone that is conspicuously absent today. Spiritual renewal is not restricted to any one gender, but the medieval Islamic world recognised the importance of cultivating strong paragons of Islamic masculine chivalry to carry the inheritance of the Prophet to its next holders. The decline of masculinity embodied by the Ummah of the Chosen One ﷺ since then has been startling.

The Modern Muslim Masculine Crisis

The rise of modern secular scepticism for ritual and the [at times compelled] Westernisation of Muslim lands led to the destruction of many of the systems of masculine spiritual initiation – the effects of which now can be seen in the Muslim world. However, to frame the recent downturn in male fortunes as a crisis that only Muslims are experiencing would be disingenuous; the Western world is arguably undergoing a comparatively worse case of gender-based maladies. Gender-dysphoria and body dysmorphia in both men and women in Western countries are but a few of the myriad issues plaguing these societies, and by extension, the Muslims residing therein. The great socio-economic changes brought by the last century and the philosophical shifts in conceptions of gender have contributed to produce a very dire situation for masculinity and femininity alike.[14]

To survey the modern masculine malaise is a dismal endeavour; an endless array of young men embroiled in what Zimbardo calls 'arousal addiction;' instead of undergoing the difficulty of carrying familial and societal responsibilities, men are now content to just engross themselves in endless hours of pornography and video-game addiction.[15] Why bear the nagging of a spouse and the crying of babies when sexual arousal without all that 'baggage' is available? This problem has been exacerbated further by the current pandemic with men flocking to social media platforms like OnlyFans for companionship at ever-increasing rates.[16] Suicides, dropping out from education and occupations, increasing rates of obesity, pursuit of criminal activity in gangs, and illegal drug use are many ways in which men in the West, and the East to a lesser degree, are crying out for help.[17] Turning to strongmen like Donald Trump and amateur pseudo-spiritual sages like Dr Jordan Peterson can be seen as another clear indicator of men trying to hold on to their traditional masculine selves in a world that wants to erode it away.

Muslim communities tend to be uniquely affected by this crisis, with their general working-class nature in the UK amplifying the effects of the socioeconomic causes further. Dr Fauzia Aḥmad, a London-based sociologist has studied what some call the 'British Muslim spinster crisis' – Muslim women have overtaken men in educational and professional life, and, in a quest to stay true to their natural desire for socially superior spouses, are not finding men to be up to par.[18] A cursory glance at crime figures in the UK shows disproportionate representation for Muslim men behind bars, and the recent unveiling of historic cases of grooming carried out by gangs of predatory men – who also happened to be Muslim – is more evidence of emerging problems within the Muslim male population.[19] This disfigurement of masculinity spells disaster for Muslims, as small local communities and the larger global Muslim family are forced to rely on spiritually deformed men for leadership. The proposed solutions are as numerous as the symptoms, divided ideologically along polarised political lines. The left's insistence on blaming society for sculpting 'toxic qualities' on to apparently blank canvases of androgyny, and the right's confinement of men to a singular, constricted, and angry stereotype of what it means to be a man are the two options available, neither of which is concordant with Islamic ethics.[20] Regrettably, Muslim attempts to address the crisis of masculinity often take the form of wholesale adoptions of Western solutions without consideration of their ideological origins.

A Model of Muslim Masculinity

To deny the material and sociological drivers of the current crisis would be foolish and disingenuous, however, a truly Islamic analysis with its proposed solutions to the ills present would utilise a deeper spiritual gaze imbued 'with the light of Allah', without being straddled by the ideological trappings of any singular politically-influenced vision of the entailments of true masculinity – rather, the Muslim understanding must be informed by a willingness to adopt wisdom regardless of its origins. It is in this vein that the sage of the British Isles, Sheikh Abdal Hakim Murad, argues that the crisis can ultimately be traced to the decline of religion and the metaphysics underlying it; an imbalance in the perception of humans has led to an emphasis on the material where the body alone is the primary 'creedal object'.[21] Modern ideas of gender are entrenched in this materialistic world-view – power structures are the primary lens by which the world is to be ordered, with clearly paradoxical results. This confusion, imbalance, and flux is the natural result of what Ibn al-Qayyim refers to as the *wahshah* – isolation; man is isolated from his Lord and is therefore, by extension, isolated from his true purpose and reality.[22] We are left floundering like fish out of water, not cognizant of the fact that true gender equality can only be achieved when each gender is allowed to flourish on its own biological terms, and only the 'ungendered logos' (Allah) can be the basis for true spiritual equality.[23] The modern masculine crisis has its own unique dynamic in this unanchored sea of secular chaos. The monomythic men's movement has identified two primary causes of the man-child we see in front of us today: the loss of rituals of initiation and the resulting absence of true father figures, both themes present in the traditional *futuwwah* literature.

Traditional Muslim communities, where the men would be at the borderlands defending the realm of Islam, recognised that fathers were not immortal and had institutions and systems in place to provide surrogates. Imam Aḥmad and Imam al-Bukhārī both grew up without fathers, but nevertheless were men in the truest sense of the word. As the world becomes individualised and our communities become more fragmented, the absence of these institutions becomes increasingly conspicuous. A process of initiation can also be clearly discerned by anyone with an eye of early Islamic History, especially when one examines the prophetic environment. The two young Companions – Sayyidunā Samurah and Sayyidunā Rāfiʿ – wrestling each other before Uhud for the right to offer their lives to the Divine, as the Chosen One ﷺ graciously inspected them, is just example of many moments of initiation that took place in that blessed environment.[24] In a beautiful article on Traversing Tradition, Ustadh Luqman Quilliam makes the case for 'a return to ruggedness' – as the lives we live become more comfortable and spiritually dull, believers should insert themselves into harsh situations in an effort to remain prepared 'for when the good-times end'.[25] Anyone with a keen eye on the Islamic eschatological literature would see that time to be very close.

The Task at Hand

Imam al-Ghazālī, when speaking about the causes of anger, points to the pseudo-masculinity of men who define their temper tantrums as 'manhood' or chivalry. The Imam is scathing; he sees this as nothing but 'ignorance, imbecility and a disease of the heart'.[26] Islam has its own framework for determining what is (or is not) toxic, entrenched in its own spiritual tradition, and it is clearly time for Muslims to return to it. Imam Dawud Walid's work in *Blackness and Islam, Towards Sacred Activism* and *Futuwwah and Raising Males into Sacred Manhood* is a commendable effort to use the Islamic tradition to provide Muslims and non-Muslims alike with the solutions to the very many social maladies present on this planet. His incredible foresight and presence at the forefront of these efforts, combined with his grasp of the Islamic tradition, make him fully qualified to address these issues. As the world descends into moral decay before the end of times, as prophesied by the Chosen One ﷺ, Muslims have been instructed to create their own pockets of resistance to the scourge of liberal consumerism and surveillance capitalism. These small pockets will strive to hold on to their faith, akin to holding a burning ember, until they would converge under the guidance of the returning Messiah. His words all miraculously chosen with meticulous intent, the Chosen One ﷺ told us that 'men from my Ummah' will meet Jesus, the son of Mary.[27] For that to happen, these men, not just males, need to be developed and institutions need to be revived. For too long has the Muslim Ummah depended on spiritually disfigured males, not men, to leads its communities, further perpetuating the crisis on the ground. Strong men are strong husbands, fathers, and are the backbone of a strong Ummah. We hope this work will be the first step in the great Muslim masculine revival, spiritually anchoring Muslims while strengthening their socioeconomic position through a philosophy founded on the ideals of Muslim Brotherliness. We pray that Allah accepts this effort from Imam Dawud Walid, and makes it the 'coolness of the eyes' of the greatest man to ever walk the face of this earth – the greatest embodiment of masculine chivalry any eye has ever seen, a father who would patch his own clothes and sweep his house, a spiritual leader who would spend long nights weeping for his people until his blessed feet would swell up, and a husband who was always in the service of his womenfolk: Our master and guide, Muhammad ﷺ, the son of ʿAbdullāh.

[Maulana] Asim Ayub
High Wycombe, Buckinghamshire, UK

Author's Preface

My reasons for writing this book emerged from my own observations in recent years, as well as those of numerous Muslim men and women in America, Canada and the UK, from whom I have heard lamenting their perceptions that the number of 'real men' among Muslims in the West is on the decline. There are different manifestations that have been observed in this regard: it is not uncommon nowadays, for instance, for young males in their twenties to shy away from responsibility. I have seen up-close countless males who have graduated college or have jobs that provide them with sufficient incomes to be able to maintain wives and start families, yet nevertheless these males are content with being single and lounging around the parents' nests. As I heard Dr. Muhammad ibn Yahya al-Ninowy once say, relating to the need for reviving virtuous, responsible manhood, that 'we do not need more males (*dhukūr*), but we need more men (*rijāl*)'. A male with a beard or a deep voice, physically resembling an adult male, does not necessarily equal a man in the traditional sense of meaning.

From the need to restore manhood due to the increase of so-called 'beta males' – meaning males who are passive and prone to be subservient to women – a troubling reaction has arisen in response:

a brutish mentality among a growing number of males who seek to rescue manhood. Some of what I have also witnessed is an overreaction of addressing one extreme of unmotivated, uncourageous males with another extreme of harsh, dogmatic males who lack social intelligence. This environment has given rise to popular Youtubers and bloggers that fashion themselves as the vanguards of true manhood. Many young men follow and cheer on such individuals because they fill a perceived void for those who feel that manhood is under assault. The irony is that many of these defenders lack proper comportment with their seniors and knowledge, even being involved in dastardly public attacks against women, which of course, is both unmanly and unchivalrous.

In Detroit, I am a part of a group led by our leader Imam Saleem Khalid, which also includes Sheikh Abdul Karim Yahya, Sheikh Ibrahim Kafani Cisse, Imam Seifullah Shakoor, Ustadh Shakir Bakari, Jermaine Carey, Khalil Mu'minun, and Jabril Ahmad, may Allah preserve them, known as the Ansar Collective. The Collective was started to implement a spiritual upbringing of young men through teaching them about sacred manhood, starting with teachings from the *Risālah al-Qushayriyyah fī 'Ilm al-Taṣawwuf* by Imam al-Qushayrī and *Kitāb futuwwah* by al-Sulamī. This book was inspired by the sessions held throughout the past three years to address the emasculation of males, offering a healthy spiritual environment and an alternative to aspects of the online 'manosphere' that lacks the spiritual comportment and emphasis of our sacred tradition.

This book is also meant to be a basic study guide for fathers with their sons, teachers with their students, and mentors with their mentees. The book, furthermore, is meant to be a supplement to a regime of embodied practice by those teaching it, further experienced in consistent organized group settings. Like my previous book *Towards Sacred Activism,* this work was written with the intention of being taught, even if remedially, to those walking the path to raise up and mentor young males to be chivalrous Muslim men. In other words, this book is in the vein of texts aiming to train the trainer. This will require readers to attend retreats, which can also include camping outings, to sit with teachers who can give commentary on this book, as works on any subject require clarifications to enable understanding and implementation – not just for the purpose of reading in gatherings to obtain blessings. In order to teach, the teacher must first be a proper student. Thus, it is my hope that this book will be used in Islamic schools, as well as serve as a basis for retreats that may one day lead to the establishment of regional *futuwwah* guilds that will also include rites of passage, organized community service, martial arts, archery, hunting, swimming, fishing, physical fitness training, and artisan training, all of which were aspects of guilds prior to the fall of the Ottoman Empire.

The Islamic tradition calls for a revival of organized training relating to spiritual chivalry and sacred manhood – this is the task of the hour.

Introduction

WITH THE NAME OF ALLAH, THE MERCIFUL BENEFACTOR, THE MERCIFUL REDEEMER

All praise and thanks belong to Allah, who is the Existence by which all that exists manifests through His will. I testify that there is no deity except Allah, who has no partner nor equal, nor is there anything which can contravene His speech and nothing that can substitute it. And I testify that our master Muhammad ﷺ is His slave-servant and messenger, the medicine of our hearts, and the light of our vision. O Allah, send prayers and peace upon our leader, Prophet and Master Muhammad ﷺ and upon the family of our leader Muhammad ﷺ, the enjoiner of good, forbidder of evil, the fountainhead of truth, and the sun of the sacred law.[28] *Peace be upon you O Master of Leaders, Imam of the People of Noble Manifestations; to you is the first and the last of majestic humanity, inward and outward honour, and all sacred manhood, loyalty, chivalry and purity.*[29]

Surely the best of speech is the Book of Allah (Qur'an), and the best of guidance is the guidance of [Prophet] Muhammad ﷺ. And the worst of matters are newly invented matters [in the religion], and every newly invented matter [in the religion] is a [blameworthy] innovation.[30] *And every [blameworthy] innovation is misguidance, and every misguidance is in the Fire.*[31]

We seek refuge in Allah from misguidance and from entering the Fire. As for what follows:

In the present era, there is a crisis of manhood in Western societies; in fact, manhood seems to be on the verge of extinction. When I say manhood, I am not primarily speaking from a physiological standpoint, even though there is a minuscule percentage of the population identifying as other than their confirmed genders at the time of birth. I am also not positing that 'manhood' is coterminous with brutish behaviour towards females, which is in fact not manly. I am speaking of manhood in terms of positive masculine energy embodied by men who are driven to compete towards excellence, embrace responsibilities, engage in self-restraint, and engage with society courageously.

Not long ago, young males who acted passively would be challenged to 'man up'. There was a time when more was expected out of young males in American society. Older men energetically encouraged young males to take on certain manly attributes. We were expected to open doors for females, carry grocery bags for ladies, and not raise our voices around elders. Our football and baseball coaches once motivated us – 'fired up; ready to go'! We went on hunting trips together, where we were taught how to use rifles responsibly. Shooting a deer to bring back food for one's family was a source of healthy pride; an example of what men are supposed to do. For others, there were activities such as cub scouts/boy scouts through which certain survival skills were taught, serving as rites of passage. Many of us who converted to Islam inherited a chivalrous code of honour similar to the Arabic code of *futuwwah* in the Era of Ignorance before Islam.[32] This America in which I grew up in, however, has been steadily fading away since the 1990s.

The decrease in manhood among males which has been discussed as a social epidemic by some, may in fact be on the verge of pandemic proportions. Dr. Leonard Sax's 2007 book *Boys Adrift: The Five Factors Driving the Growing Epidemic of Unmotivated Boys and Underachieving Young Men,* broached this topic from a secular, sociological viewpoint. His diagnosis of the crisis argues that the predominance of school environments (which lack men as teachers and role models), an overprescribing of psychotropic medications for ADHD, environmental factors (which have negatively affected young males' hormone levels), and the devaluing of traditional masculinity, have all led to the decline of strong, productive men in Western societies. Though not speaking only about young males, the 2018 work *The Coddling of The American Mind: How Good Intentions and Bad Ideas Are Setting Up a Generation for Failure,* elaborates on the issues of 'safetyism' and 'overprotectionism', arguing that they have led to loss of resiliency among many men of an entire generation. These are all psychosocial factors that have ushered in today's crisis of manhood in the West.

In addition to the general point about the devaluing of traditional masculinity, the gender confusion movement has effectively normalized gender dysphoria in the West. How can one even talk about traditional manhood when once-positive aspects of masculinity, such as warriorhood and protectiveness, have been redefined as 'toxic masculinity' – much less when masculinity has been redefined as in a manner divorced from physiology? A non-hermaphrodite female can say that she feels like a man, and that is supposed to be accepted by all in the public sphere, even when this goes against the overwhelmingly predominant understanding of what defines a man in the history of human civilization. A non-hermaphrodite male, conversely, can state that he feels like a woman. Male roles and expectations are being stripped away in the age of postmodernism; a female or a male can claim to not have a gender at all, defining themselves as agender or genderfluid (a conception in which the person can supposedly morph into a gender-shapeshifter, similarly to Thetis in the Greek myth *Iliad,* who changed from a lady into a sea nymph). The sexual and gender confusion movements, which have incessantly promulgated their messages in pop culture and the activism world, have made their way into public school classrooms of young folk who have not even reached the age of puberty, lacking the cognitive capacities to process these matters with critical thinking skills.

Muslims who live in the West are influenced by the socio-political trends surrounding them. The issues of seemingly unmotivated young males and unproductive twenty and even thirty-something-year-old man-children are phenomena that are on the rise in the United States, Canada, and in the United Kingdom. Young ladies are far outpacing young men academically, including in rates of graduation from colleges and universities. In many local and national youth groups and college organizations like Muslim Students' Associations (MSA), sisters usually outnumber brothers – in some cases grossly outnumbering them. Sisters looking to get married are also having extreme difficulty finding husbands, not only because some brothers are marrying outside of the Muslim community, but also due to a widespread lack of interest in taking on the responsibility of getting married among Muslim men. Many of these 'momma's boys' who suffer from an extended psychosocial adolescence are quite comfortable with not seriously planning to take on the responsibility of maintaining families; some of them are simply too glued to their Xbox's for such considerations.

The Prophet Muhammad ﷺ said, 'For every malady, there is a remedy.'[33] At a cursory glance, the cure for the issues mentioned earlier is to institute the inverse of what has caused the problems. Adolescent males require environments affirming their masculinity to be put into place with the objective of teaching manhood. Training programs that teach resilience are needed, as are summer camps to get youth away from overprotective parents so that life skills, including conflict management, can be developed. Mentorship is a must. So-called smartphones, gadgets, and video games need to be drastically decreased in usage, while physical activities such as wrestling and martial arts, archery, and swimming (sunnah activities) should be robustly encouraged, although they require mass organized instruction. Time and sweat must be spent by men to organize such activities, and doing so should take precedence in our community fundraising efforts, more so than multimillion-dollar houses of worship that may end up being empty within less than twenty-five years at the rate that some communities are declining.

To be even more explicit, the Islamic tradition calls for a revival of organized training relating to spiritual chivalry and sacred manhood – this is the task of the hour. There are beautiful and majestic qualities embodied by the Prophet ﷺ that he passed down to his family members and pious Companions. Those upright men were methodically raised up: they undertook rites of passage, and manly responsibilities which were placed upon them with expectations that they would be executed with excellence. We must expect more from our young men if we expect to see a healthier, more productive manhood emerge in the generations to come.

In this vein, *Futuwwah and Raising Males into Sacred Manhood* will concisely discuss the principles within spiritual chivalry that we should strive to inculcate as men and teach to the young males in our communities. While the virtues that will be discussed are not all exclusively regarding young males becoming men, this book is tailored towards males. Part of the problem with postmodernism is the discourse that gender differences and separation need to be completely torn down. Just as young ladies need their own spaces to learn from women how to become honourable sisters, young men require their own special places to instil in them the virtues of upright brothers. I believe, as it relates to the latter gender, that the community should start to organize *futuwwah* guilds in particular localities for young men to have such special places.

Though this book is informed by my upbringing and what has been displayed to me by the comportment (*adab*) of my teachers including my current *murabbī*, the contents were primarily drawn from the books and treatises of *futuwwah* that were taught and passed down in our Islamic heritage. The first of these books is *al-Futuwwah,* by Muhammad ibn al-Ḥusayn al-Sulamī رحمه الله, a scholar of the 4th

Hijri century who was the first to compile a specific book on this topic. Following him in this endeavour was the Ḥanbalī scholar Muhammad ibn al-Miʿmār ﵀ with his book carrying the same name. Sheikh Aḥmad ibn Muhammad ibn Mīkā'īl al-Ardabīlī also authored a book with the same title. Other scholars who wrote chapters and treatises about *futuwwah* include Sheikh Al-Qushayrī in *al-Risālah Al-Qushayriyyah,* Ibn Qayyim al-Jawziyyah in *Madārij al-Sālikīn,* ʿAbd al-Razzāq al-Qāshānī in *Tuḥfah al-Ikhwān fī Khaṣā'is al-Fityān,* and ʿAbdullāh al-Anṣārī al-Ḥanbalī, who wrote a commentary on al-Qāshānī's work entitled *Manāzil al-Sā'irīn.* These are the primary – but not exclusive – references used in this work.

The methodology of this book is to relay essential virtues for developing healthy manhood in a specific order after elaborating on linguistic and operational definitions of *futuwwah.* The Prophetic narrations and sayings of the pious Companions ﵃ are relayed with a sound meaning, trusting that the scholars of *futuwwah* were taught them based upon the Qur'anic ethos. I did not list the full chains of narrators in this book except in one case, nor did the authors of specific books on *futuwwah* list chains of transmission for most of the Prophetic sayings, with the exception of al-Sulamī. Moreover, some of these sayings have been graded as 'weak' in chains of transmission according to some hadith scholars, especially when it comes to *marāsīl* reports that are either missing narrators, or simply stated that the Prophet ﷺ said such and such, or Ḥasan al-Baṣrī ﵀, the famous scholar of the second generation of Muslims, said that the Prophet ﷺ said such and such. Such deficiencies, however, do not detract from the correctness in meanings of such reports. As scholars from earlier generations such as Imam Aḥmad ibn Ḥanbal ﵀ conveyed that 'weak' hadith narrations with meanings that encourage virtuous actions are permissible to relay and act upon.[34]

May Allah ﷻ guide us to better follow the complete example of our master Prophet Muhammad ﷺ. May He increase us in love for his immaculate household and his rightly guided Companions. May He have us stick to our spiritual guides, and may He present to us guides for those of us who do not have them in our lives at this time. May He set the affairs of the Muslim youth aright and cause them to be among the transmitters of this noble path. May Allah forgive me, forgive you, and forgive all Muslims.

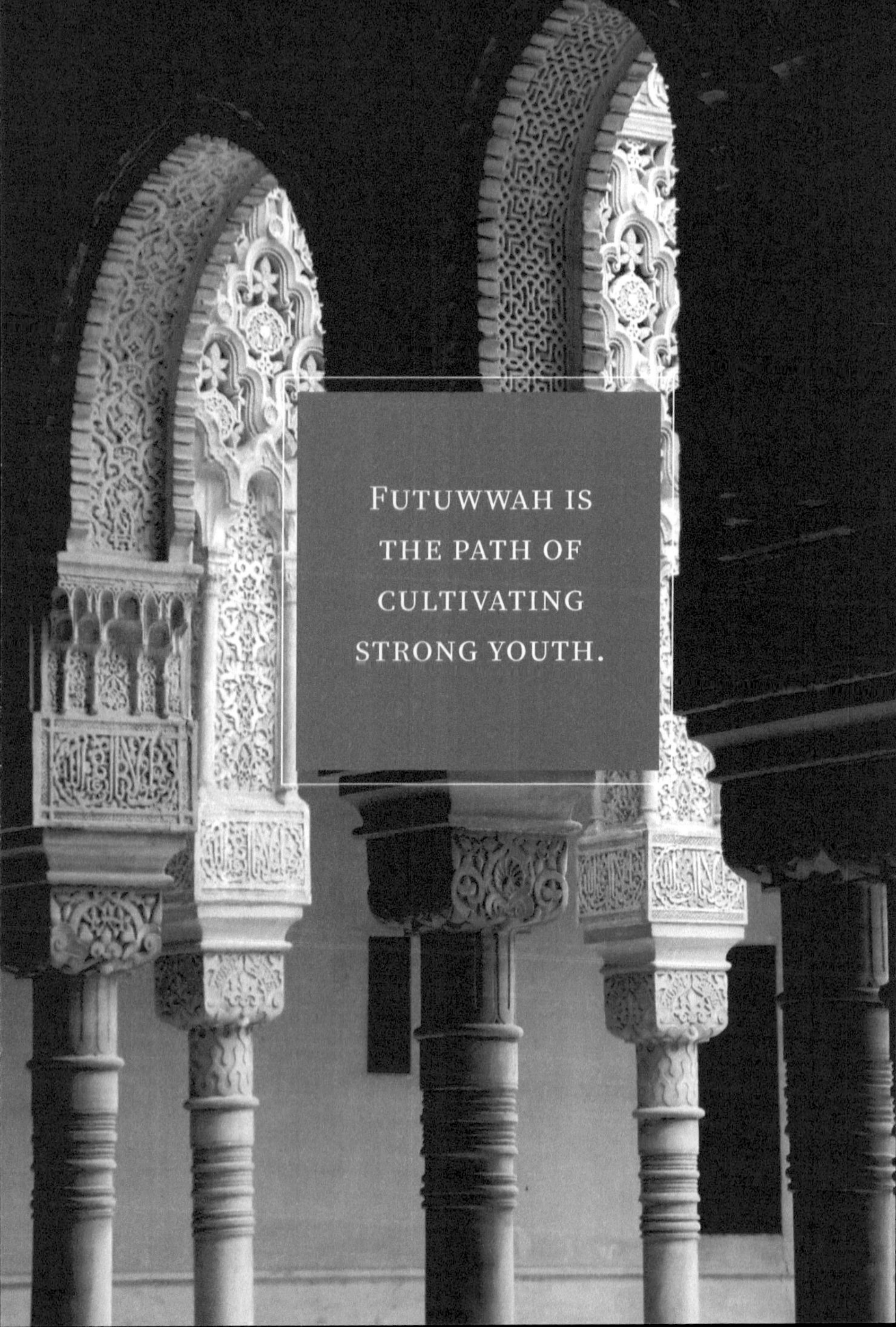
FUTUWWAH IS
THE PATH OF
CULTIVATING
STRONG YOUTH.

What is **Futuwwah?**

Futuwwah linguistically derives from *fa-ti-ya,* meaning to be youthful.[35] It is related to the word *fatā* meaning a young male, and *Fityān* being a gathering or group of youth. *Fatā* is understood from the aspect of age to be one in between the period of early teens and manhood.[36] It connotes the meaning of a youth moving from one stage of life to another, or transitioning from adolescence into an age of a youth having greater maturity. This transitioning into a stage of greater maturity, of course, does not equal entering into the stage of wisdom displayed by elders, just as Yazīd al-Raqāshī stated that youthfulness displayed by elders is a despicable trait.[37] *Fatā* can also carry the meaning of a slave, or one who serves another who is superior in social rank.[38] This is conveyed operationally when Prophet Muhammad ﷺ stated, 'None of you should call anyone "my slave", for all of you are slaves of Allah. Instead say, "my youngster"..."my *fatā* "'.[39] *Futuwwah,* moreover, has a relationship with the term *fatwā,* meaning to make a judgement or verdict on an issue of importance.[40]

Futuwwah cannot be simply defined operationally speaking, as although it is loosely translated as spiritual, chivalry in the English language is defined as characteristics of a distinguished gentleman or a knight who displays courage, honour, courtesy, justice, and a readiness to help the weak. Not only does the term have a shade of elusiveness in giving it one rigid definition, but there are also differences of opinion as to when the term came into usage among the Arabs. In essence, *futuwwah* is the outward exemplification of an inward code of honour.

Al-Ardabīlī wrote in *Kitāb al-Futuwwah:*

> And certainly, Allah Most High mentioned *futuwwah* in His glorious book in seven instances. He praised every station of it with elaboration and veneration. Such is the speech of the Most High in *Surah Yūsuf* [in verse 30], '*And some women gossiped in the city, "The wife of the chief minister is trying to seduce her fatā (enslaved young man)."*' Allah described his innocence and praised his mindfulness, as he chose Him over his desires; thus, He named him *al-fatā*.
>
> Second, in *Surah Yūsuf* [in verse 62], the Most High said, '*And he (Yūsuf) told his fityān (his young servants) to put the money of his brothers back in their saddlebags so that they can find it when they return to their family so that they may come back.*' And Allah Most High knows of their trustworthiness and conviction; thus, He named them *al-fityān*.
>
> Third, in *Surah al-Kahf* [in verse 10], the Most High said, '*Remember when those fityah took to the cave and said, "Our Lord!"*' Allah Most High knew their innermost selves, so He purified their residency since they were searching for Divine mercy and sought to perfect their faith; thus, He named them *al-fityān*.
>
> Fourth, also in *Surah al-Kahf* [in verse 13], the Most High said, '*They were fityah who believed in their Lord, and We increased them in guidance.*' This was without intermediaries or physical demonstrators. Of course not, they believed in Him and [struggled] for Him; thus, they were honoured with an increase in guidance so that they rose to a noble place.
>
> Fifth, in that same surah [in verse 62], the Most High said, '*When they passed further, he (Mūsā) said to his fatā, "Bring us our meal.*' Allah knew he was sympathetic in his friendship and excellent in

companionship; thus, He named him *al-fatā*.

Sixth, in the same surah [in verse 60], the Most High said, '*Remember when Mūsā spoke to his fatā.*' Allah selected him for his excellent example and protective, loving affection; thus, He named him *al-fatā*.

Seventh, in *Surah al-Anbiyā'* [in verse 60], the Most High said, '*They said, "We heard a fatā named Ibrāhīm speaking [ill] of them [meaning the idols]."*' Allah Most High praised His friend with honour, mindfulness, truthfulness, and loyalty; thus, He named him *al-fatā*.[41]

It was narrated that Ḥasan al-Baṣrī said, 'The conglomeration of *futuwwah* is in [*Surah al-Naḥl*, verse 90] the speech of the Most High: *Surely Allah enjoins justice and goodness, giving to close kin, prohibits immorality, evil and rebellion. He admonishes you in order that you may be heedful.*'[42]

It is narrated that Imam Jaʿfar al-Ṣādiq[a] relayed from his father who relayed from his grandfather that Prophet Muhammad said:

> There are ten signs of the *Fityān* of my community.
>
> It was asked: O Messenger of Allah. And are there *Fityān* from your community now?
>
> He replied: Yes. And where is the foremost of *futuwwah* from the *futuwwah* of my community?
>
> The questioner then asked: And what are their signs, O Messenger of Allah?
>
> He said: They are those who are truthful in speech, loyal in oaths, who fulfil their trusts, abandon lying, are merciful with the orphans, give to whomsoever asks [for help], spend on the one

---

a   Imam Jaʿfar ibn Muḥammad al-Baqīr ibn ʿAlī Zayn al-ʿĀbidīn ibn al-Ḥusayn ibn ʿAlī ibn Abī Ṭālib is listed as an Imam in the spiritual chains of transmission of the Bāʿalawī, Qādirī, Rifāʿī, Naqshbandī, and Khalwatī spiritual orders.

> who has, are generous with the craftsman and with guests, and the head of them is one who is modest.[43]

The Mother of the Believers, 'Ā'ishah ﷺ also narrated a similar hadith. Imam 'Alī ibn Abī Ṭālib ﷺ stated, 'The best traits of the *fatā* are courage and generosity, and both of these come together in the generous valiant one.'[44] Along a similar vein, it is narrated by Imam 'Alī Zayn al-'Ābidīn[b] ﷺ that he said, 'the *fatā* is one who does not hoard, nor is impractical.'[45]

Ma'rūf al-Karkhī [c] ﷺ said, 'the signs of the *fityān* are three: Loyalty without breaching it, giving without being asked, and praising without being shown generosity.'[46] Sheikh Abū al-Ḥusayn al-Warrāq proposed five divisions of *futuwwah*:

> The foundation of *futuwwah* is in five qualities: The first of these is guardianship, the second is loyalty, the third is gratitude, the fourth is patience, and the fifth is contentment.[47]

Sheikh Sahl ibn 'Abdullāh al-Tustarī said, '*futuwwah* is following the Sunnah.'[48] Likewise, Imam Muhammad ibn al-Ḥanafiyyah[d] ﷺ said, '*Futuwwah* is obedience to the One that he is enslaved to.'[e]

Referring to the seven sections in the Qur'an that make specific

---

b Imam 'Alī Zayn al-'Ābidīn ibn al-Ḥusayn ibn 'Alī ibn Abī Ṭālib was from the 2nd generation of Muslims and was a notable teacher of the Islamic sciences in Madinah after the martyrdom of his father in Karbala, Iraq. He is an Imam in the spiritual chains of transmission of the Bā'alawī, Qādirī, and Rifā'ī spiritual orders and is considered the 4th infallible Imam of the Twelver Shia.

c Ma'rūf al-Karkhī was an early ascetic of Muslim community who converted from Christianity at the hand of Imam 'Alī al-Riḍā' ibn Mūsā ibn al-Kāẓim ibn Muḥammad al-Baqīr ibn 'Alī Zayn al-'Ābidīn. He is listed in the chain of transmission of the Qādirī spiritual order.

d Imam Muhammad ibn al-Ḥanafiyyah was one of the sons of Imam 'Alī ibn Abī Ṭālib. He is known as ibn al-Ḥanafiyyah due to his mother having been a Sindhi servant of the tribe of Ḥanīfah.

e Al-Kasnazān, Mawsū'ah al-Kasnazān fīmā Aṣṭalaḥa 'Alayhi Ahl al-Taṣawwuf wa al-'Irfān, vol. 17, p. 229.

reference to *fatā*, *fityān* and *fityah*, Ibrāhīm ☙ is the first to be named as being on the chivalrous path. Al-Qāshānī mentioned that *futuwwah* is sticking to the sound Abrahamic primordial nature that the Most High referred to in *Surah al-Shuʿarāʾ*, verse 89:[49] *'Except whom Allah has given a sound heart.'*

The way of *futuwwah* was displayed in varying aspects and circumstances by the Prophets and saints who came after them. The exemplification of the chivalrous path then manifested in the descendant of Ibrāhīm ☙, with the answer to his prayer being Prophet Muhammad ☙. The Most High said regarding the Seal of the Prophets, Prophet Muhammad ☙, in *Surah al-Qalam*, verse 4, *'And surely you are upon a magnificent character.'*

Imam Zayd ibn ʿAlī[f] ☙ said that this verse means that the Prophet ☙ was established upon the Qurʾan and Islam.[50] This carries the meaning that the Prophet's ☙ primordial nature never departed from the soundness of heart required to embody the Qurʾan to the fullest possible extent of human potential. The way of *futuwwah* was then bequeathed from the Prophet ☙ to Imam ʿAlī ibn Abī Ṭālib ☙, whom Al-Ardabīlī referred to as *Master of the Fityān*.[51] Furthermore, he was described as 'our leader in knowledge of the spiritual path and its embodied actions' by the great chivalrous ascetic al-Junayd al-Baghdādī ☙.[52]

Prior to Imam ʿAlī reaching the age of puberty, his upbringing was supervised by the Prophet ☙, as he lived with the Prophet ☙ in his residence.[53] He was the first to submit and believe in the Messenger of Allah ☙ from the male population of Makkah, after Sayyidah Khadījah ☙ accepted Islam.[54] He was also the first person to perform prayer with the Prophet ☙.[55] Imam Aḥmad ibn Ḥanbal ☙ stated that

---

f Imam Zayd ibn ʿAlī bin al-Ḥusayn bin ʿAlī ibn Abī Ṭālib was a gnostic and scholar of the early generations of Muslims and teacher of Imam Abū Ḥanīfah for a duration of two years. He was martyred in Kufah, Iraq, decapitated just as his grandfather Imam al-Ḥusayn was martyred and decapitated in Karbala, Iraq.

none from among the generation of Companions had more sound hadith narrated about their virtues than Imam ʿAlī.[56] Imam ʿAlī's virtues were not simply from his own independent merit, but were an extension of a spiritual inheritance transferred to him.

One of the indications of this spiritual inheritance is displayed in an incident in which a group of Christian scholars from Najrān came to the Prophet ﷺ to discuss religious issues, as they disagreed with the prophetic position on the status of ʿĪsā ﷺ. This is the context of the revelation of *Surah Āl ʿImrān*, verse 61, which says:

> *And whoever disputes with you in this matter after what has come to you of knowledge, then say: 'Come, let us call our sons and your sons, and our women and your women, and ourselves and yourselves, then let us earnestly invoke the curse of Allah upon the liars.'*

When the Prophet appeared with his daughter Fāṭimah, his grandsons al-Ḥasan and al-Ḥusayn ﷺ and Imam ʿAlī, the Christians declined to invoke curses upon the liars then departed. al-Shaʿbī[g] stated as it relates to this verse:[57]

> 'Our sons' means al-Ḥasan and al-Ḥusayn ﷺ, 'our women' means Fāṭimah, and 'ourselves' means ʿAlī ibn Abī Ṭālib ﷺ.

Al-Ḥākim also interpreted the exact same indications from this verse.[58] Hence, part of the secret of Imam ʿAlī is his being described as from the self or soul of the Prophet ﷺ.

Another such indication is apparent in an event in which the Prophet ﷺ wore a black cloak in which his grandsons al-Ḥasan and al-Ḥusayn entered under it, followed by his daughter Fāṭimah and

---

g Al-Shaʿbī was from the second generation of Muslims and was a student of Imam ʿAlī, as well as Jābir ibn ʿAbdullāh and other prominent Companions.

Imam ʿAlī. After they were all wrapped in the cloak with the Prophet ﷺ, he recited from *Surah al-Aḥzāb*, verse 33: 'Allah but desires to remove impurity from you, O People of the House, and thoroughly purify you.'[59] This is symbolic of the spiritual investiture conferred from the Prophet ﷺ to Imam ʿAlī.

In two famous narrations, the Prophet ﷺ said, '[For] whoever I am his master, then ʿAlī is his master', and told him, 'You are in the position to me as Hārūn was to Mūsā.'[60] It is reported that he also stated, 'There is no sword except Dhū al-Fiqār, and there is no *fatā* except ʿAlī.'[61] Al-Suhrawardī[h] relayed that he also stated to ʿAlī:[62]

> 'Oh ʿAlī, Go to this man's house and look around well!' Now, there is a question here: Why did he send Ali and not any other person? [Why] did he send Bilāl for other tasks, and ʿAlī for this [particular] task? The answer is that no one possessed the same [degree of] knowledge as ʿAlī. Anyone else [sent by Muhammad] would have seen and would have testified [to the situation] just as it was. But ʿAlī was greater than all the others in knowledge and more famous through futuwwah – since the Prophet had stated 'there is no *fatā* but ʿAlī, and there is no sword except Dhū al-Fiqār.'

Ibn al-Miʿmār stated that the saying 'there is no *fatā* except ʿAlī' is a statement of amplification, carrying the meaning that 'there is no complete *fatā* except ʿAlī'.[63] Hence it was also relayed that the Prophet ﷺ proclaimed that 'The most chivalrous of you is ʿAlī'.[64]

Hence, *futuwwah* is characterized by the process of transferring spiritual qualities (which are embodied in conduct) from a master to his disciples. When the disciples come into maturity – not simply in age, but in striving towards self-mastery – they in turn pass the

---

h Shihāb al-Dīn ʿUmar al-Suhrawardī was a Persian ascetic who lived during the rule of the Abbasid ruler Al-Nāṣir li Dīn Allah. Although his most famous work about spiritual purification (entitled *ʿAwārif al-Maʿārif*) was written in Arabic, he wrote a treatise in Farsi titled *Kitāb fī al-Futuwwah*.

mantle of chivalry to the next generation of disciples. The uprearing of such disciples necessarily includes rites of passage (or initiation) within sacred spaces, to which young males travel to be among the *fityān*. In his treatise *Kamāl al-Murū'ah fī Jamāl al-Futuwwah,* Ibn Ṭūlān describes the dressing of disciples in the clothing of *futuwwah,* passed down along the following chain:

> My father dressed me with the above-mentioned [clothing] in our lodge in Nablūs al-Maḥrūsah. He said, 'I was dressed by Rāḍī al-Dīn Abū Bakr ibn Ibrāhīm ibn Maḥmūd al-Ḥumayrī al-Kalā'ī al-Yamanī in Masjid al-Aqṣā in the month of Jumādā al-Ūlā in 749 AH.' He said, 'I was dressed by Burhān al-Dīn Abū Isḥāq Ibrāhīm ibn 'Umar ibn Ibrāhīm al-Ja'bārī, Sheikh of the Tomb of Al-Khalīl (Prophet Ibrāhīm) ﷺ.' And he said, 'I was dressed by Sheikh Tāj al-Dīn Muhammad ibn Sheikh Shams al-Dīn Muhammad ibn Sulṭān al-'Ārifīn Muḥyī al-Dīn Abī al-'Abbās Aḥmad ibn Abī al-Ḥasan 'Alī ibn Aḥmad al-Rifā'ī.' And he said, 'I was dressed by 'Imād al-Dīn Ismā'īl Nāqib al-Ashraf, the famous Khāṭīb of Wāsiṭ.' And he said, 'I was dressed by the Commander of the Faithful, the Khalīfah al-Mustanṣir bi Allāh.' And he said, 'I was dressed by the Commander of the Faithful, al-Ẓāhir bi Allāh.' And he said, 'I was dressed by Abū Ya'qūb, who is famously known as al-Aṭṭār.' And he said, 'I was dressed by 'Abd al-Jabbār.' And he said, 'I was dressed by Salmān al-Fārisī.' And he said, 'I was dressed by 'Alī ibn Abī Ṭālib ﷺ, the nephew of the Messenger of Allah ﷺ.' And this is the mode of transmission of the dressing during which a sheikh dresses his disciple.[65]

The way of *futuwwah,* as expressed within guilds, was also a characteristic of the government of the Abbasid Khalīfah Al-Nāṣir li Dīn Allah ﷺ when confronting the Crusaders.[66] Al-Nāṣir li Dīn Al-lah was a renaissance man, dressed in the robes of *futuwwah* and well-studied in Prophetic traditions prior to ascending to the seat of governmental authority, from which he established these guilds. In fact, as it relates to his connection to traditional transmission, he compiled a book of hadith in which he relayed full chains of narration entitled *Ruḥ al-ʿĀrifīn min Kalām Sayyid al-Mursalīn*. As these guilds established by Al-Nāṣir li Dīn Allah were centred on modelling noble traits of character, these brotherhoods also trained and organized their members in the art of defence on behalf of the Muslim community.

Futuwwah is the path of cultivating strong youth.[67] Strength is not merely an aspect of physicality, but arises from virtuous qualities that are exemplified in individual behaviour and fortified through organized brotherhood. Those raised on the path are guided to selflessness rather than self-absorption, courage in the face of immorality (as well as imminent threats to physical safety) rather than cowardice, distaste of harm coming to anyone, and disdain of revelling in the misfortunes of others – including adversaries. Within this framework, the following chapters will touch on specific traits vital for raising up young males embodying spiritual chivalry.

"TRUTHFULNESS
IS THE CLOTHING
OF CERTITUDE."

Truthfulness

Truthfulness is an essential quality of the chivalrous path and it is the foundation from which all noble traits of character extend from. Truthfulness is related to the primary trait that the Arabs referred to Prophet Muhammad ﷺ in the Era of Ignorance before the revelation of the Qur'an; he was known as the Truthful (*al-Ṣādiq*) and the Trustworthy (*al-Amīn*).[i] Sheikh al-Jazūlī mentioned that he was known by his contemporaries as such, because his truthfulness was seen to be lofty – or even exaggerated – compared to what was common among them.[68] From a linguistic perspective, truthfulness (*ṣidq*) is informing others of an event exactly as it occurred, with its meaning standing as the opposite of falsehood.[69] Allah ﷻ said in *Surah Āl 'Imrān*, verse 61:

> *And whoever disputes with you in this matter after what has come to you of knowledge, then say: 'Come, let us call our sons and your sons and our women and your women and ourselves and yourselves, then let us earnestly invoke the curse of Allah upon the liars.'*

---

i Truthfulness was a quality embodied by all Prophets and Messengers. The impeccable truthfulness of Prophets and messengers gave initial credibility to these men to convey Divine glad-tidings and warnings, and to legislate sacred law to their nations. That Prophet Muhammad ﷺ was unanimously known among the Arabs in the Hijaz during his lifetime as being truthful and trustworthy, which made it incumbent upon them to believe in the message that he conveyed, and exposed the hypocrisy of those who did not sincerely follow him.

The Prophet ﷺ reportedly said regarding this, that 'whoever desires that he invokes curses upon himself is lying.'⁷⁰ The Prophet ﷺ also stated:

> Surely truthfulness leads to righteousness, and surely righteousness leads to Paradise. And surely a man keeps on telling the truth until he becomes a truthful person. Surely falsehood leads to evildoing, and surely evildoing leads to the Fire, and surely a man may keep on telling lies until he is written to be a prolific liar.⁷¹

Imam ʿAlī ibn Abī Ṭālib ؓ said, 'Truthfulness is the strongest of the pillars of faith.'⁷² He also stated that 'the truthfulness of a man is based upon the measure of his manhood',⁷³ and that 'There is no manly nobility for a consistent liar.'⁷⁴ Likewise, Sheikh Al-Qāshānī mentioned that the beginning point of truthfulness in the path of chivalry and manhood lies in one's intentions, and that truthfulness is in one's integrity of purpose being directed to Allah, The Most High.⁷⁵ Thus the Most High said in *Surah Fuṣṣilāt*, verse 6, *'Therefore, stand true to Him.'*

When Mūsā ؓ reportedly asked about *futuwwah*⁷⁶, Allah ﷻ replied: [*Futuwwah*] is that you return your soul to Me pure, just as I accept from Myself being pure. Speaking of the importance of pure intentions, the Prophet ﷺ said:

> Actions are but by their intentions, and everyone shall get but what they intend. Whoever migrates for the sake of Allah and His Messenger, then his migration is for Allah and His Messenger. And whoever migrates for worldly gain or to marry a woman, then his migration is for the sake of what he migrated for.⁷⁷

In a similar narration, the Prophet ﷺ also reportedly stated, 'The intention of the believer is better than his action, and the intention of the corrupt person is worse than his action.'⁷⁸ The saints and scholars of the following generations expounded upon the importance of pure intentions, as Imam ʿAlī said, 'A righteous intention is one of the two actions.'[79] Furthermore, Imam Mūsā al-Kāẓim ﷺ said, 'Just as the body does not stand without a living soul, the religion does not stand without truthful intention.'[80] So too did Sheikh Ibrāhīm ibn Adham[j] ﷺ say, 'Sincerity is truthfulness in intention with Allah, the Most High.'[81]

Speaking of the centrality of intention, Sheikh ʿAbdullāh ibn al-Mubārak stated, 'Many an action is big, but lessened by its intention, while many an action is small, but made great by its intention.'[82] Likewise, Sheikh ʿUmar al-Suhrawardī said, 'intention is the deed of the heart',[83] and Sheikh Muhammad al-Darqāwī stated:

> There is nothing more beneficial for you, O poor one, than truthfulness with your Lord in what He commanded you and in what He prohibited you. By Allah, if you are like this with Him, you shall see wonders [in your life]. Remember that Allah, the Most High, said in *Surah Muhammad*, verse 21, '*If they had been truthful with Allah, surely it would have been better for them.*' By Allah, if we are truthful with Him, He will be truthful with us [aiding us] against our enemies.[84]

The second level of truthfulness, as mentioned by Al-Qāshānī, lies in speech.[85] Imam Yaḥyā ibn Ḥamzah al-Dhammārī ﷺ stated that truthfulness in speech is that which relates to information connected to the past or the present.[86] Moreover, Imam ʿAlī said, 'Truthfulness is the trust of the tongue and the adornment of faith'[87], and that 'truthfulness is the clothing of certitude.'[88]

---

j Ibrāhīm ibn Adham was from the third generation of Muslims. He was born in Balkh, which is in present day Afghanistan. He was known as a leading gnostic and ascetic of his era, as well as being a narrator of prophetic traditions. He learned under great scholars such as Sufyān al-Thawrī and al-Fuḍayl ibn ʿIyād, and was one of the teachers of the famous ascetic Shaqīq al-Balkhī.

Imam Zayd ibn ʿAlī ﵁ stated, 'The right of the tongue is keeping it clean from deceptive speech, falsehood, and profanity, and that you use it to establish truth for the sake of Allah without fearing vile criticism.'[89] Likewise, Sayyid ʿAbd al-Qādir al-Jīlānī[k] said, 'Truthfulness in speech is the placement of mindful speech in its appointed time.'[90]

A famous story relating to the demonstrated truthfulness of Sayyid al-Jīlānī's words illustrates this virtue: when he left his home as a teenager to study in Baghdad, his mother had him pledge a vow that he would never tell a lie. He then departed with forty gold coins in his possession. During his travels, he was ambushed by a group of bandits. One bandit said to him, 'O poor one, what do you have with you?' Sayyid al-Jīlānī replied, 'Forty gold coins.' The bandit asked, 'Where is it?' He told the bandit that it was sewn into his jacket pocket, upon which the bandit thought that he was joking. Another bandit came to him and asked the same question, to which he gave the same reply. After searching his clothes, this bandit found the forty gold coins. He asked Sayyid al-Jīlānī why he informed him of his gold coins, to which he responded, 'Surely my mother had me promise that I would always tell the truth, and I cannot break my promise to her.' The bandit began to weep, then said, 'You did not break your promise to your mother, but surely I, on this day and in this year, broke my promise to my Lord.' Thereupon, the bandits repented for their crimes after witnessing the truthfulness of Sayyid al-Jīlānī.[91]

This well-known event of Sayyid al-Jīlānī is a testament to the high degree of truthfulness that a *fatā* can exhibit. He was foremost truthful in front of Allah ﷻ in his oath to be truthful at all times, even

---

k Sayyid ʿAbd al-Qādir al-Jīlānī, who lived between 470 AH and 561 AH, was Hanbali polymath that authored texts of the exegesis of the Qur'an, Islamic jurisprudence, spiritual purification, and futuwwah. He was a descendant of Prophet Muhammad ﷺ through Imam al-Ḥasan ibn ʿAlī in his paternal lineage and Imam al-Ḥusayn ibn ʿAlī in his maternal lineage. He is one of the most revered spiritual doctors in Islamic circles after whom the Qādirī spiritual order was named. He is entombed in Baghdad at the famous mosque named after him.

Surely truthfulness leads to righteousness, and surely righteousness leads to Paradise. And surely a man keeps on telling the truth until he becomes a truthful person. Surely falsehood leads to evildoing, and surely evildoing leads to the Fire, and surely a man may keep on telling lies until he is written to be a prolific liar.

in adversity. His truthfulness extended to not breaking the promise that he made to his mother, although she was not physically present. He also was truthful with those who were wronging him, embodying the lesson that the *fatā* should not be dishonest with people even when they violate his own rights. This embodiment of truthfulness was a means by which Sayyid al-Jīlānī was protected from harm, and by which those who were in misguidance were guided aright. This is a magnificent lesson for today's young males, showing how true empowerment comes from a sincere devotion to the truth.

Al-Qāshānī mentioned that the third level of truthfulness relates to truthfulness in actions.[92] Truthfulness in actions also relates to keeping one's trust. Allah ﷻ said in *Surah al-Aḥzāb*, verse 23, *'From among the believers are men who are true to what they pledged to Allah.'* Along a similar vein, Allah ﷻ stated in *Surah Yūnus*, verse 2, *'And give good news to the believers that they will have the status of truthfulness with their Lord.'* Commenting on this, al-Qāshānī said, 'Whoever is not truthful, there is no portion for him in *futuwwah*. Of course not, [as] his demeanour is unbecoming of manhood.'[93]

Some of the disbelievers among the Quraysh trusted the Prophet ﷺ with their property. Upon his migration from Makkah to Madinah, he left Imam ʿAlī behind in Makkah to return their property and goods to them.[94] Likewise, when the Prophet ﷺ instructed his most vulnerable Companions to migrate from Makkah to Abyssinia, he told them, 'Go to the land of Abyssinia, for surely it has a king who does not wrong anyone. It is the land of truth. Stay there until Allah makes for you relief in what you are in.'[95]

The Prophet ﷺ referred to Abyssinia as the land of truth in relation to the righteous al-Najāshī, Aṣḥamah ibn Abjar ؓ[1], whose ac-

1 Aṣḥamah ibn Abjar, ruler of the Aksumite Empire of Greater Ethiopia – also known as Abyssinia (al-Ḥabasha). He was known by his title of the Negus (al-Najāshī), an honorific for the emperors of the Ethiopian Kingdom. More can be read about al- Najāshī in the book *The Spirits of Black Folk: Sages Through the Ages*, which is a translation by Sheikh Adeyinka Mendes and

tions were sincere and conformed to truth and justice. His sincerity in intentions, words, and actions were further confirmed when he heard the message of the Qur'an, after which he converted from Christianity to Islam. His son, nephew, and other righteous Abyssinian Jews and Christians followed him into Islam, through which the practice of Islam was established in Abyssinia before reaching Iraq, Syria, and Yemen.

ʿAbdullāh ibn ʿAbbās ﷺ said, 'There are four characteristics that whoever has them will prosper: Truthfulness, modesty, good character, and gratitude.'[96] Accordingly, Sayyid al-Jīlānī stated that it is said that truthfulness is loyalty to Allah by one's actions,[97] and Sheikh Abū Nājib al-Suhrawardī reportedly said, 'The station of truthfulness is loyalty for the sake of Allah [displayed] through actions.'[98]

Ustadh Talut Dawood, of al-Suyūṭī's book *Rafʿ al-Sha'n al-Ḥubshān* published by Imam Ghazali Publishing.

"Whoever loves and loathes for the sake of Allah, and gives and refuses for the sake of Allah, most certainly perfects his faith."

Loving and Loathing **for the Sake of Allah**

The *fatā* who is truthful on the path both loves and loathes for the sake of his Creator. In relation to this, Sheikh Dāwūd al-Ṭā'ī ﷺ defined love as permanence and persistence in remembering the object of love.[99] Offering another opinion, Sheikh Shāh al-Kirmānī said that love is preferring the desires of the object of love [to one's own], and loving the beloved of the object of love.[100]

Imam Aḥmad al-Rifā'ī ﷺ said, 'The root of love is annihilation.'[101] This carries the meaning that the lover annihilates his own desires when they are nonconcordant with the object of his love. Similarly, Sheikh Aḥmad al-Kubaysī, may Allah preserve him, stated that 'love is the opposite of vain desire, in that love, which is attached to the heart, is not blameworthy, whereas vain desire, which attaches to the heart, is not praiseworthy'.[102]

Imam al-Rifa'i also stated that love is blindness of the eye from other than the object of love and is the uprooting of that which equals it in the heart.[103] The Prophet ﷺ stated in this regard, 'Whoever loves and loathes for the sake of Allah, and gives and refuses for the sake of Allah, most certainly perfects his faith.'[104] Given that love and faith pertain to the heart, the *fatā's* striving to perfect his love for Allah ﷻ requires that he attaches himself inwardly to whatever Allah ﷻ says that He loves. As Sheikh 'Abdullāh ibn 'Alawī once stated, 'Love of

Allah, the Most High, is inclining towards, attaching to, and allying with Him.'[105]

Thus, Allah ﷻ said in *Surah al-Baqarah*, verse 165, *'And among the people are those who take others for worship instead of Allah, loving them as Allah should be loved. But those who believe are strongest in their love of Allah.'* Imam ʿAlī ibn Abī Ṭālib ؓ commented on this, saying, 'The most knowledgeable of the people with Allah are those who are strongest in their love [for him].'[106] Sayyid ʿAbd al-Qādir al-Jīlānī also stated:

> O young man! Love of the Truth ﷻ and love of other than Him cannot come together in one heart. Allah Most High said [in *Surah al-Aḥzāb*, verse 4], *'Allah did not make two hearts in the chest of any man.'*[107]

Loving Allah ﷻ relates to knowing Him, for it is not possible for anyone to love without knowing the object of that love. Allah ﷻ stated in *Surah al-Dhāriyāt,* verse 56: *'And I did not create jinn nor men except that they worship Me alone.'* Imam al-Qāsim al-Rassī ؓ commented on this verse, stating:

> Worship is sectioned off upon three parts: The gnosis (maʿrifah) of Allah, the knowledge of what pleases Him and what displeases Him and following what is pleasing to Him and staying away from what displeases Him.[108]

It has been relayed that Imam ʿAlī prayed:

> It suffices me in dignity that You are my Lord to me, and it suffices me in honour that I am to You a slave. You are to me just as I love, so help me conform to what You love.[109]

One cannot conform to what Allah ﷻ loves without obedience to His commands; as Aḥmad ibn Abī al-Ḥawārī stated, 'a sign of loving

Allah is obeying Allah'.[110] Likewise, Sheikh Dāwūd al-Kabīr ibn Mākhilā said, 'Whoever loves Allah, the Most High, loves all of what exists as means to Him.'[111] Thus, it is incumbent upon the *fatā* to learn the beautiful, majestic, and perfect names of Allah ﷻ, to constantly remember Him – an act which includes being in the company of those who will remind him of God, and learning the basic obligations and prohibitions of the sacred law.

It is narrated that Allah ﷻ revealed to Dāwūd ﷺ the following words: 'Surely whoever knows Me wants and desires Me. And whoever desires Me, he will find Me. And whoever finds Me, he will not find over Me an object of his love equal to Me.' [112] As it relates to loving Allah ﷻ, the *fatā* cannot be consumed with love of this world (*dunyā*). The Prophet ﷺ said, 'Renounce the world, and Allah will love you. Renounce what people possess, and people will love you'.[113] Renunciation of the world (*zuhd*) means emptying one's heart of it while possessing it in one's hand (i.e. restraining one's usage of it and not letting it control the person). The spiritual journey of the *fatā* leading to closeness with Allah ﷻ is a journey of emptying his heart of love for everything save Allah ﷻ, one in which the youth loves to adorn himself with love of Allah and what He loves.

Ḥasan al-Baṣrī ﷺ said, 'Whoever knows that Allah loves him, and whoever knows the world, renounces it.'[114] Dāwūd al-Ṭā'ī ﷺ advised one of his disciples to 'fast from the world and make your breaking of the fast the Hereafter'.[115] Ibn Abī al-Ḥawārī stated, 'Whoever knows the world, renounces it.'[116] Some of the wisemen have also proclaimed:

> The world is [nothing] but desire for three [goals]: dignity, wealth, and repose.
> Whoever renounces it gains dignity.
> And whoever is content in it is wealthy.
> And whoever abandons running after it finds repose.[117]

When it comes to loving what Allah ﷻ loves, there is nothing in creation more beloved to Him than the Prophet ﷺ, who said of himself that 'I am the beloved of Allah'.[118] This is confirmed in *Surah al-Aḥzāb,* verse 6, where Allah ﷻ states that 'The Prophet is closer to the believers than their own souls'. The Prophet ﷺ proclaimed, 'None of you will ever believe until I am more beloved to him than himself, his wealth, and his children',[119] and in a similar narration, he ﷺ stated, 'None of you believes until I am more beloved to him than his parents, his children and all of the people.'[120]

This love for the Prophet ﷺ was present in the hearts of the following generations, such that when Imam ʿAlī was asked, 'How is your love for the Messenger of Allah?' he replied: 'By Allah, he is more beloved to us than our wealth, our sons, our daughters, our mothers, and cool water in a time of great thirst.'[121] The Prophet ﷺ is the best of Allah's creation, exemplifying all noble character traits which Allah ﷻ stated that He loves in the Qur'an, confirmed by Allah ﷻ in *Surah al-Aḥzāb*, verse 33: *'Most certainly you have been given in the Messenger of Allah a beautiful example for whoever believes in Allah, the Last Day, and remembers Allah often.'*

In his quest to increase his love for the Prophet ﷺ, the *fatā* must connect himself with gatherings of the learned and pious scholars who teach the traits of the Prophet ﷺ and remember him. When any person falls in love, they thirst to know more about the object of their love; the more any person loves another, the more that they long to be in their presence. Such feelings of love and longing must be actualized in the *fatā*'s love for the Prophet ﷺ. Thus, he should frequently read the Shamā'il about his physical appearance, beautiful characteristics, and habits.

Allah ﷻ said in *Surah Āl ʿImrān*, verse 31, *'Say [O Prophet]! "If you love Allah then follow me, and Allah will love you and forgive you of your sins. And Allah is Oft-Forgiving, the Merciful Redeemer"'.* Thus, the *fatā* should have an internal yearning to have his desires conform with whatever the Prophet ﷺ instructed him to do or what he ﷺ inclined towards, for doing so is a sign of his love for his Creator. This internal yearning is part of the meaning of al-Tustarī's statement that '*futuwwah* is following the Sunnah.'[122] Accordingly, the *fatā* should also send frequent Ṣalawāt upon the Prophet ﷺ every night and day, acting upon the enjoinment of Allah ﷻ in *Surah al-Aḥzāb* verse 56: *'Surely Allah and His angels send Salah upon the Prophet. O you who believe! Send Salah upon him and salute him continuously with peace.'*[m]

Frequently sending Ṣalawāt upon the Prophet ﷺ contains many benefits, one of which is raising the spiritual station of the one[n] who sends Ṣalawāt upon him often with loving or longing for him in the heart, as well as fortifying one's connection with the Prophet ﷺ. It is beneficial for the *fatā* to make a part of his daily litany at least 1000 Ṣalawāt every day, including ten Ṣalawāt after his Fajr and Maghrib prayers, for the Prophet ﷺ stated, 'Whoever sends Ṣalāt upon me ten times at the time of dawn and ten times at the time of dusk shall be granted my intercession on the Day of Resurrection'.[123] It is an added benefit for the *fatā* to increase his Ṣalawāt on the night and day of Jumu'ah, giving special attention to the practice in the first Jumuʿah night of the sacred month of Rajab, as well as sending Ṣalawāt upon him eighty times during on the day of Jumuʿah before leaving the prayer hall following ʿAṣr prayer.

The *fatā* must also know that his sincere love for the Prophet ﷺ has a price attached to it, and that its payment comes through standing firm upon his way, through both tests and malignment from those who disbelieve in him – as true love is accompanied by tests.

---

m Ibn 'Abbās said, 'The meaning (of this verse) is that Allah and His Angels bless the Prophet.' It has also been said that it means, 'Indeed, Allah has mercy upon His Prophet, and the Angels supplicate for him.' Al-Mubrid said, 'The root meaning of ṣalāh (prayers) is to show mercy. Thus, (prayers) from Allah are mercy and prayers from the Angels are compassion and seeking for Allah to have mercy (on the person).' This was referenced from *On Prayers Upon the Prophet ﷺ (Gems from the Shifa of Qadi Iyad)* translated by Ustadh Talut Dawood.

n Abū Bakr Al-Qushayrī said, 'The prayer of Allah (Exalted is He) upon other than the Prophet ﷺ is mercy, while His prayer upon the Prophet ﷺ is an ennoblement and an increase in honour.'

Indeed, Allah ﷻ informed us of this in the second and third verses of *Surah al-ʿAnkabūt*:

> *Do people think that they will be left alone by saying 'We believe' and not be tested?*
>
> *And We certainly tested those who came before them; Allah will clearly distinguish those who are truthful from those who are untruthful.*

Along this vein, it is reported that a man allegedly once came to the Prophet ﷺ and said, 'Surely, I love you for the sake of Allah ﷻ.' He responded, 'Take tests as your cloak; take poverty as your cloak.'[124]

Due to his love for Allah ﷻ, the *fatā* loves the Prophet ﷺ, and through his love for him, he loves the Prophet's family. Allah ﷻ said in *Surah al-Shūrā*, verse 23, *'Say [O Prophet!] 'I ask no reward from you except loving my close kin.'* Sayyid ʿAbd al-Qādir al-Jīlānī ؓ explained that, at the occasion of this verse being revealed, it was asked, 'O Messenger of Allah, who are your close kin?' He replied, ''Alī, Fāṭimah, and their two sons [al-Ḥasan and al-Ḥusayn].'[125] Al-Ṭabarānī ؓ narrated a similar narration regarding this question posed by the Prophet's Companions: [it was asked] *'Who are your close kin those whom it has been made obligatory upon us to love them?' The Prophet ﷺ replied, 'Ali, Fāṭimah, and their two sons [al-Ḥasan and al-Ḥusayn.]'*[126]

When Imam al-Ḥasan ibn ʿAlī ؓ gave a sermon after the martyrdom of his father, he praised and thanked Allah ﷻ, then preached:

> I am al-Ḥasan, the [grand]son of Muhammad, may Allah's prayers and peace be upon him and his family. And I am from the People of the Household, those to whom Allah ﷻ has made love for and spiritual allegiance to them obligatory. This is what was revealed to Muhammad, may Allah's prayers and peace be upon him and his family, regarding this: 'Say [O Prophet!] "I ask no reward from you except loving my close kin."'[127]

When ʿAlī ibn al-Ḥusayn ibn ʿAlī ibn Abī Ṭālib ﷺ was brought to Damascus as a captive following the massacre of his father, brothers, uncles, cousins, and his father's Companions at Karbala, the following transpired:

> A Syrian man said: All praise belongs to Allah He who killed and eradicated you, cutting off the kin of fitnah.
>
> ʿAlī ibn al-Ḥusayn replied: Do you read the Qur'an?
>
> The Syrian responded: Yes.
>
> ʿAlī ibn al-Ḥusayn asked: Have you read about the family of *Ḥā-Mīm*?
>
> The Syrian replied: I read the Qur'an, but have not read about the family of *Ḥā Mīm*!
>
> ʿAlī ibn al-Ḥusayn asked: Have you not read 'Say [O Prophet!] I ask no reward from you except loving my close kin'?
>
> The Syrian inquired: Are you among them?
>
> ʿAlī ibn al-Ḥusayn replied: Yes.[128]

In another narration, ʿAlī ibn al-Ḥusayn also said, 'Love of us is love of Islam for the sake of Allah'.[129] Thus, the Household of the Prophet ﷺ should be loved, and their descendants should be respected due to their connection to the Beloved. Sayyid ʿAbd al-Qādir al-Jīlānī wrote on this topic, commenting 'his [the Prophet's] household is the most honourable of households, his family is the most virtuous family, and dignity and homage have been established for them by his side'.[130]

Among his descendants through Imam al-Ḥasan and Imam al-Ḥusayn are honourable men and women who embody and transmit the sacred law and Islamic spirituality, in which reverence from them is due. If the *fatā* finds any of his descendants involved in open immoral behaviour, he should act especially kind to them for the sake of the Prophet ﷺ, and he should pray for their guidance, neither reviling them nor praying against them.

An example of this was reported in the story of a *sharīf* (meaning a descendant of Imam al-Ḥasan) who lived in Khurāsān yet unabashedly committed major sins in public, and a black sheikh, who, while a mere slave (and certainly not a *sharīf* according to lineage), was so obedient to Allah ﷻ that his master freed him.[131] Many people would come to the black sheikh looking for blessings (*tabarruk*) while they stayed away from the *sharīf*. One day, the *sharīf* approached the black sheikh in a state of intoxication, as people came to him for blessings (which included kissing him). The *sharīf* then told the black sheikh:

> You are a black man, son of a black disbeliever; my grandfather is the Messenger of Allah ﷺ. Your grandfather was a disbeliever; you are praised and exalted, while I am censured and treated lowly by the people.

The black sheikh replied:

> Yes, I am the son of a disbeliever just as you said, and I am black just as you said, but my heart has been illuminated with faith in Allah ﷻ and *taqwā*. Thus, the people see my heart as white above my black face, and so they love me. Though I am the son of a disbeliever, I left the path of my father and follow the path of your father, the Messenger of Allah ﷺ. You left the path of the Messenger ﷺ, and follow the path of my father, so your heart has blackened due to corruption and disobedience. Thus, the people see your black heart over your white skin, and so they loathe you because they see you on the path of my father.

We can thus see how the black sheikh gave the *sharīf* a truthful response without cursing him for his public intoxication, hoping that the *sharīf* would return to the way of his most noble ancestor, the Prophet ﷺ. Like this noble character, the *fatā* should also love the Prophet's righteous Companions for his sake, for loving them is a sign of loving the Prophet ﷺ and loving him is a sign of loving Allah

☙. The Prophet ﷺ stated 'Surely, Allah Most High has commanded me to love four men and informed me that He loves them: 'Alī is among them, as are Abū Dharr, al-Miqdād, and Salmān.'[132]

Abū Dharr and al-Miqdād ☙ were Arabs, but not from the tribe of Quraysh, whereas Salmān ☙ was Persian. Salmān was of the clients (*mawlā*) of the Prophet ﷺ, and was manumitted from enslavement by him, thus receiving his protection. The Prophet ﷺ said, 'Salmān is from us, the People of the Household.'[133] Ibn 'Aṭā' Allah al-Iskandarī ☙ said, 'It is well-known that Salmān was from Persia, but he was spiritually related to him [the Prophet].'[134] He also proclaimed, 'Whoever loves Allah and His Messenger should thus love Usāmah ibn Zayd'.[135] Like Salmān, Usāmah's parents were both under the cliental protection of the Prophet ﷺ, his mother having been the Abyssinian noble Umm Ayman ☙, bringing Usāmah into the Prophet's clan.

The *fatā* should also sincerely pray the supplication attributed to Dāwūd ☙:

> O Allah, Surely, I ask you for Your love, love for whoever you love, and deeds which bring me Your love. O Allah, make Your love more beloved to me than myself, my family, and cool water.[136]

"Learn for
yourselves,
then teach
goodness to your
families."

Vigilant Care

Islamic chivalry and sacred manhood must contain the quality of vigilant care *(ghayrah),* which is sometimes described as protective jealousy. This vigilant care relates to the recognition of someone or something worthy of protecting based upon its essence, and it carries the opposite meaning of selfishness, for one cannot have vigilance over another if he is only concerned about himself.[137] If the *fatā* is sincere in his love, he must have healthy protective jealousy for the objective of his love. The Prophet ﷺ said:

> Surely Allah cares vigilantly, the believer cares vigilantly, and the protective jealousy of Allah is provoked when a believer commits what is forbidden.[138]

He also stated:[139]

> None has more protective jealousy than Allah ﷻ, and that is regarding that which He has made forbidden of acts of indecency and lewdness, both [those done] openly and [those] hidden. And none loves to be praised more than Allah ﷻ, and that is how He has praised Himself.

Imam ʿAlī ibn Abī Ṭālib ؓ said, 'The protective jealousy of the believer is in Allah, Glorified is He.'¹⁴⁰ He also stated, 'The vigilant care of a man is faith.'¹⁴¹

The *fatā* is to protect himself from transgressing the limits set by Allah ﷻ. Likewise, he must have vigilant care for the Qurʾan, such that he does not mock any of its contents openly or secretly. Moreover, he must be prepared to defend the honour of Allah's book if, or when people openly make a mockery of it or deliberately subvert its clear, declarative meanings. If the *fatā* lacks the knowledge or the permission required to openly defend the honour of the Qurʾan through words and acts of non-violence (such as protests), his protective jealousy means that, at the least, he completely despises disrespect towards Allah ﷻ. The one who lacks this fundamental trait like one who has a physical heart that beats while his spiritual heart needs resuscitation. When Hudhayfah ibn al-Yamān ؓ was asked about the meaning of 'the one who is the dead among the living', he replied that it is 'whoever does not recognize good in his heart, and does not despise wrong in his heart'.¹⁴²

The *fatā*, in his love for the Prophet ﷺ, is to also have protective jealousy relating to him. He is not to transgress the authenticated commands and prohibitions of the Prophet ﷺ, for it is clearly written in *Surah al-Nisāʾ*, verse 80 that *'whoever obeys the Messenger most certainly has obeyed Allah'*. In his vigilant care for the Prophet ﷺ, he must prepare himself to defend his honour from those who seek to disrespect his words and actions, or ridicule him in the public sphere.

Just as the *fatā* is to have protective jealousy relating to Allah ﷻ, His book and His final Prophet – which is vigilant care for Islam itself – he is also to have such vigilance over his family.¹⁴³ Ibn ؓ mentioned that an essential meaning of vigilant care is that a man is vigilant over his family. This is taken from the meaning of *Surah al-Taḥrīm*, verse 6: *'O you who believe, save yourselves and your families from the fire whose fuel has men and stones.'*

“Just as the *fatā* is to have protective jealousy relating to Allah ﷿, His book and His final Prophet – which is vigilant care for Islam itself – he is also to have such vigilance over his family.”

Imam ʿAlī ibn Abī Ṭālib said in reference to this verse, 'Learn for yourselves, then teach goodness to your families.'[144] The meaning of this includes teaching proper comportment through words and actions, as well as instructing them in sacred knowledge. If, perchance, the *fatā* becomes more scholastically learned in sacred knowledge than his parents, his teaching them should be done through demonstration, more so than exhorting good verbally. This is the way in which Imam al-Ḥasan ibn ʿAlī and Imam al-Ḥusayn ibn ʿAlī, still youths at the time, allegedly taught an elder the proper way of making Wuḍūʾ when he was making mistakes: instead of teaching him with words, they taught him by properly making Wuḍūʾ in front of him then asking him if their Wuḍūʾ was correct.[145]

Imam al-Sayyadī said that, pertaining to one on the path of spiritual wayfaring, he is obligated to have fervour and vigilant earnestness (*ghayrah*) for Allah Most High and His Messenger, and is thereby obligated to have love for everyone who loves Allah and His Messenger.[146] This should translate into having a sense of vigilant care for the religion of Islam, such that the *fatā* should not be indifferent when he sees the religion being mocked, irrespective of whether disbelievers are doing so or misguided Muslims who disrespect and make a mockery of the sacred law and revered Islamic landmarks. In fact, it is meritorious for the *fatā* to have a sense of righteous indignation when he sees the religion being ridiculed or attacked, although he must show temperance in how he responds.

The vigilant care that the *fatā* should have for his family is to protect them from potential physical harm. If he gets married, this means protecting his wife; if he is not able to marry, this should be in his consciousness, considering the future responsibility they may have if Allah grants him a wife from His provisions. Ibn Manẓūr mentioned this in his defining the meaning of vigilant care is that a man has protective jealousy regarding his wife.[147] This protective jealousy relates to his sacred duty conferred upon him in *Surah al-Nisāʾ*, verse 34: *'Men are the protecting servers of women'*. The meaning of this is that husbands are morally obliged to serve their wives, and a portion of this is to physically protect them from harm. Protective jealousy, however, becomes blameworthy if a man is verbally or physically abusive to his wife by yelling at her, calling her names, hitting her, or treating her like a prisoner in her home, by, for instance, not allowing her to visit her family, in the name of protecting her from outside harm. This is not from sacred manhood, as the *fatā* should not desire harm for anyone, especially his wife, regarding whom he has been entrusted to protect from harm, including harm which could come from himself.

The opposite of a man who has healthy protective jealousy is the effeminate, emasculated male (*dayyūth*) who is passive and shows no protective jealousy. Sheikh al-Miʿmār ﷺ said that an effeminate male cannot have sound *futuwwah*.[148] He does not have the strength to defend Islam or his family, as he allows disrespect of those whom he is supposed to protect, to the degree of letting his wife consort with other men. The Prophet ﷺ remarked that such a person will not enter paradise, along with the one who severs ties with his parents and the woman who outwardly imitates men.[149]

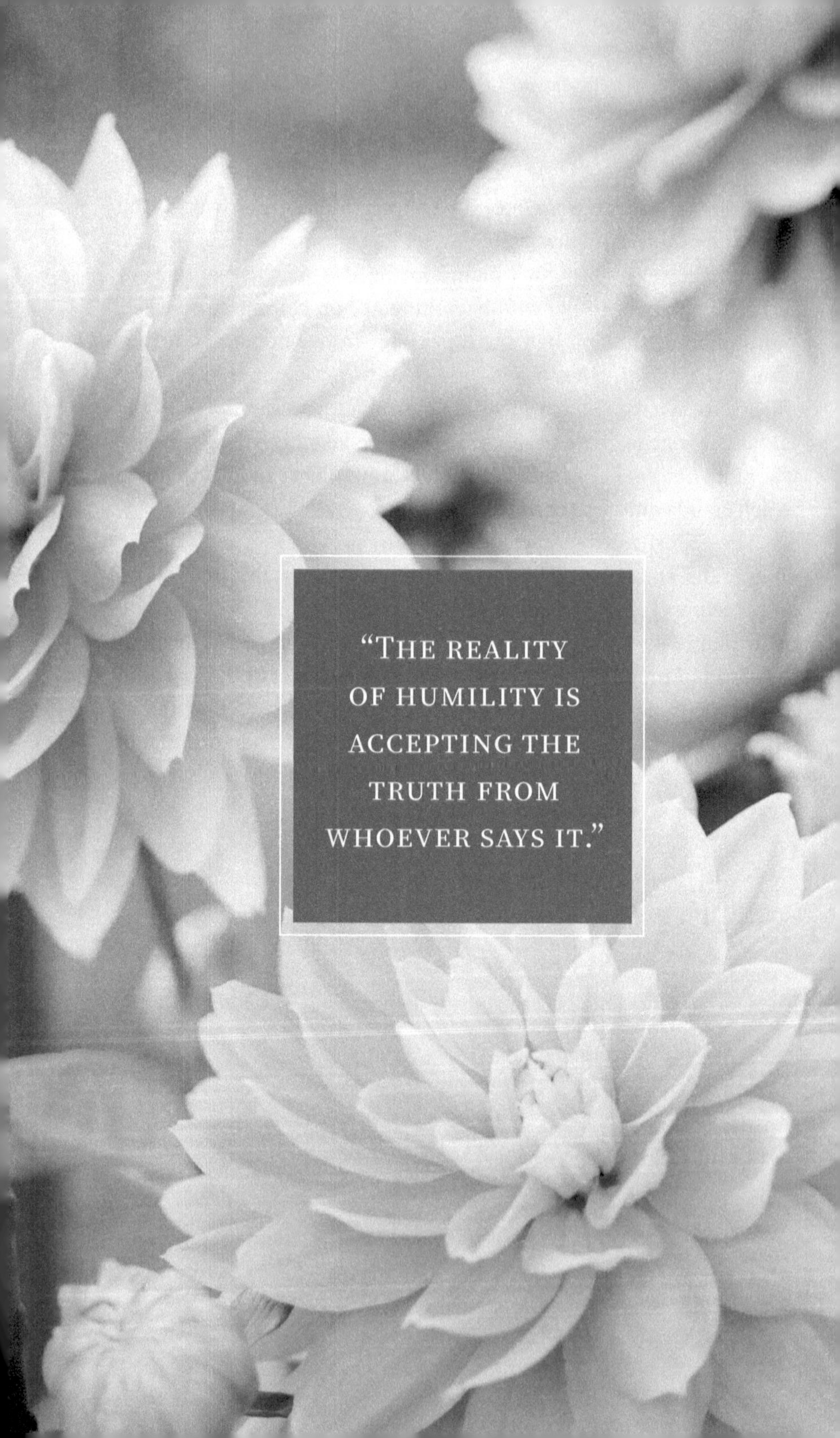

"THE REALITY OF HUMILITY IS ACCEPTING THE TRUTH FROM WHOEVER SAYS IT."

Humility

The cultivation of humility is an essential part of the spiritual path for the *fatā*. This is especially true in this era, in which people are prone towards ostentatious behaviours while posting on (anti)-social media platforms. This ranges from many young people – and unfortunately too many of their unwise elders – gloating online about every worldly accomplishment or accolade received to showcase wealth and the ability to get so-called VIP access to certain socio-political figures, at times even showing off access to religious scholars. Some are even bold enough to utter arrogant statements such as 'they are not on my level'.

Linguistically, the humility is to be inwardly submissive and outwardly subdued, and it is the opposite of arrogance.[150] Imam ʿAlī ibn Abī Ṭālib ﵁ stated that humility is that one gives to people what he loves to be given, meaning respect and deference.[151] Abū al-ʿAbbās al-Qaṣṣāb al-Ṭabarī ﵀ said, '*futuwwah* is that you do not see yourself as being superior over others.'[152] Al-Fuḍayl ibn ʿIyād[o] ﵀ relayed the same as it relates to chivalry and humility.[153]

---

o Al-Fuḍayl ibn ʿIyād was formerly a notorious bandit who made repentance one night after hearing the recitation of a verse of the Qur'an that touched his heart. He was from the 3rd generation of Muslims (Tābiʿ Tābiʿīn), a student of Imam Jaʿfar al-Sādiq and later a teacher to other notable men of futuwwah, such as Bishr al-Ḥāfī and Ibrāhīm ibn Adham.

The humblest was Prophet Muhammad ﷺ both inwardly and outwardly. He told his Companions, 'Do not exceed in extolling me just like the Christians did with 'Īsā ibn Maryam. I am but a slave, so say [about me that I am] "a slave of Allah and His Messenger"'.[154] Christians exceeded the limits in worshipping 'Īsā ﷺ, whereas the Prophet ﷺ instructed his Companions explicitly not to do. However, the Prophet ﷺ allowed his family members and Companions, such as his uncle al-'Abbās and Ḥassān ibn Thābit, to publicly recite poetry about his noble character and merits although they were forms of praise.

The Prophet ﷺ said, I am the master of the children of Adam, but [I say this] with no pride'.[155] The Prophet ﷺ also told his Companions, 'None of you should say that I am better than Yūnus ibn Māttā.[156] This proclamation exudes humility, as, of course, he is the leader of all Prophets and Messengers, those being the best of the children of Adam ﷺ whom Allah ﷻ has chosen over all other humans.

Imam 'Alī inherited the quality of humility from the Prophet ﷺ. It is narrated that his son Muhammad ibn al-Ḥanafiyyah ﷺ asked him who was the best of the people after the Messenger of Allah ﷺ in which he reportedly responded, Abū Bakr, then 'Umar, then 'Uthmān. When his son inquired, saying 'then you?', he reportedly answered, 'I am nothing but a common man from among the Muslims'.[157] This is a statement of humility as well, given the many meritorious statements that the Prophet ﷺ said about Imam 'Alī, including those giving him glad-tidings that he was explicitly guaranteed paradise.

The *fatā* should also accustom himself to avoid using 1st personal pronouns (I, me, my and mine) as much as possible in his speech. The avoidance of using these with the tongue should help in diminishing arrogance within the heart. Iblis in his arrogance was caught up in 1st person pronouns as *Surah Ṣād*, verse 76 relayed: *'He (Iblīs) said, "I am better than him (Adam), You made me of fire while You made him from the dirt."'* Furthermore, Fir'awn, the very archetype of arrogance in a human being, said as conveyed in *Surah al-Nāzi'āt*, verse 24: *'He said, "I am the most high lord."'*

Besides verbal humility, another expression of this virtue is to sit with common people and the poor, without thinking oneself to be too good to do so. This is a quality that the *fatā* has been instructed to follow. Anas ibn Mālik said that a woman came to the Prophet ﷺ saying to him, 'Surely I have a need to discuss with you.' He replied, 'Sit alongside any road in Madinah that you wish [to sit on], then I will sit with you.'[158] The woman's name was not mentioned in the narration, which leads to the understanding that she was not a person of high societal ranking, nor a famous person. If she had been well-known, it is presumed that her name would have been mentioned.

The Prophet ﷺ would also keep daily company with the poorest of people in Madinah who were homeless that slept in a special section in al-Masjid al-Nabawī. These men were known as People of the Veranda; among them were the likes of Salmān al-Fārisī and Abū Dharr ؓ who wore poor-quality, simple garments made of wool. A man reportedly came to the Prophet ﷺ one day and said:

> Most certainly I am annoyed by the smell of Salmān the Persian. Make for us a gathering with you but do not make us gather with him. Make for them their own sitting without making us sit with them.[159]

Allah ﷻ then revealed *Surah al-Kahf,* verse 28: *'And keep yourself content with those who call upon their Lord in the morning and evening, seeking His countenance, and do not turn your eyes away from them.'* The Prophet ﷺ then said, 'All praise belongs to Allah, who made in my Ummah he whom I was commanded to keep myself content with him'. 'Him' meant the poor, formerly enslaved Persian, Salmān, who was of the most honourable of the Companions.

Furthermore, the Prophet ﷺ would accept invitations of the enslaved and formerly enslaved and eat what they ate while sitting on the ground. He never saw himself too good to accept invitations nor required a special chair or throne while in the presence of the poorest of his Companions including the formerly enslaved. The Prophet ﷺ instructed Abū Dharr to 'love the poor and sit with them'.[160] Such was a reminder for Abū Dharr, who was once impoverished himself, not to forget where he came from and to remain humble.

Similarly, it has been relayed that Jaʿfar ibn Abī Ṭālib ؓ loved the poor, kept company with them, and conversed with them; thus the name Father of the Poor was bestowed on him due to this virtue.[161] Unlike Abū Dharr, Jaʿfar was from what was considered aristocracy of that era, as he was from the Quraysh and Banu Hāshim. Social status, however, did not make Jaʿfar become arrogant.

The *fatā* should strive to dress humbly. If he can wear high-quality clothing, he should not be overly extravagant in this regard. The Prophet ﷺ wore simple clothing and looked indistinguishable from his Companions. When visitors came to him who had not seen him in person before, they could not tell who he was, as kings of old wore special robes and crowns, yet the Prophet ﷺ wore no ornate rings or plush robes. He dressed simply and only adorned his finger with a silver ring with an Abyssinian stone. It is not fitting for the *fatā* to try to imitate the trends of contemporary rappers who wear overpriced clothing, platinum necklaces, and diamond rings and 'grills', even if these are not explicitly forbidden according to the *madhhab* of his parents. Bakr ibn ʿAbdullāh stated that if you 'wear the clothing of kings, then fear [of Allah] will die in your hearts.'[162] The same principle also should apply to the *fatā* regarding transportation, and he should shun flashy cars with rims more expensive than other cars.

Likewise, the *fatā* should guard his heart from wearing simple clothing or garments that exude an aura of religiosity, or from walking with the swagger of arrogance and feigned piety. This is the meaning of the ascetic Sulaymān al-Darānī when he said, 'When you see a Sufi choosing to wear simple wool clothing, he is not a Sufi'.[163] One of the trials of our times lies in young men from middle class and upper-middle class economic backgrounds who wear turbans, shawls and thawbs with ostentation. Showing off by trying to look rich or by clothing oneself in a veneer of outward piety is not true humility on the path.

An aspect of humility is the ability to accept the truth when it comes, no matter the social status of the bringer of truth. Sheikh Ibn 'Aṭā' al-Adamī said, 'humility is the acceptance of truth from any person',[164] while Imam Al-Qushayrī stated that 'humility is the acceptance of truth with beautiful character'.[165] He also stated that 'the reality of humility is accepting the truth from whoever says it'.[166]

The ultimate reality of humility pertaining to both one's inward state and his/her outward words and deeds was summarized by Abū Yazīd al-Bisṭāmī ﵀ in his statement that 'the humble person does not see the evil or wrongdoing of himself in others'.[167] As the humble man knows his own sinful thoughts, words, and deeds, and assumes those whom he comes into contact with are not as sinful in their private intentions as he is.

The people of service are those who seek to break their egos.

Service
Towards Others

A necessary consequence of the humility of the *fatā* is that he should render himself in service (*khidmah*) to others. Linguistically, service is to stand up to fulfil the need of another.[168] Thus, the servant (*khādim*) is one who stands up for the service of other than himself, whether the person is male or a female.[169] Service can range in many forms, from driving others to various locations when they visit one's locality, running errands for another person, cleaning bathrooms at institutions or houses of worship, to standing as a bodyguard to protect people or locations.

The Western philosophy of servant leadership[p] is to a degree congruent with Islamic teachings, as per the well-known principle narrated that 'a leader of a people is their servant'.[170] As a youth, the Prophet ﷺ served his uncle Abū Ṭālib. As a mature man, he served his wives, children, close kin, and Companions. If anyone asked him of something they needed, he never refused to serve anyone regarding that which was lawful.

Among those who served the Prophet ﷺ was Anas ibn Mālik: Anas was a *fatā* who served the Prophet ﷺ for a decade, happily do-

---

p Servant leadership is a philosophy in which the leader serves those who (s)he leads by uplifting and empowering them, while being humble instead of exerting authority through dictating orders and acting superior.

ing chores and errands for him.¹⁷¹ Likewise, ʿAbdullāh ibn Masʿūd ؓ - one of the earliest Muslims to convert in Makkah - performed service for the Prophet ﷺ by taking care of his shoes and cleaning them.¹⁷² Allah ﷻ raised his status to the degree that, in maturity, he was known to be of the most knowledgeable jurists among the Companions. Another companion, ʿUqbah ibn ʿĀmir, served to the Prophet ﷺ by taking care of his mule and guiding it during his travels.¹⁷³ Notably, Bilāl al-Ḥabashī ؓ served the Prophet ﷺ as the *muadhdhin*, a role which included awakening him for Fajr prayer.¹⁷⁴ Another Abyssinian, Ayman al-Ḥabashī ؓ, would regularly serve the Prophet ﷺ by getting his water for *wuḍūʾ* and *ghusl,* also tending to other needs of the Prophet ﷺ.¹⁷⁵

ʿAbdullāh ibn ʿAbbās ؓ was a *fatā* who also served the Prophet ﷺ by bringing water to him to make *wuḍūʾ*, after which the Prophet ﷺ prayed for him 'O Allah, give him deep comprehension of the religion'.¹⁷⁶ Allah ﷻ elevated the status of Ibn ʿAbbās through his service such that he later became known to be the 'Interpreter of the Qurʾan'.

Sheikh Aḥmadou Bamba^q ؓ became known to be the Servant of the Prophet (*khādim al-rasūl*) based upon a dream he had of the Prophet ﷺ, which led the sheikh to exclusively dedicate much of his life to writing Arabic poetry singing the praises of the one whom he served, extolling his noble qualities. The sheikh stated, 'Service is worship, and customs are specific to worship.'¹⁷⁷ Thus, he viewed not only the norms of ritual prayers as worship, but also the ways in which one serves others - according to what is proper in their locality - for the sake of Allah ﷻ.

The comportment of the *fatā* while in service entails not seeing

---

q Sheikh Aḥmadou Bamba, who lived between 1853 C.E. to 1927 C.E, was a Mālikī scholar and gnostic from Senegal. His mother, Sayyidah Maryam Bousso, is a descendant of the Prophet's grandson Imam al-Ḥasan ibn ʿAlī. He led a non-violent revolution against French colonial rule in Senegal that led the French to exile him to Gabon, then Mauritania. He is the founder of what is now Senegal's 2nd largest city, Touba, which was inspired by a dream in which the Prophet ﷺ came to him.

those who are being served as less virtuous than himself, showing the utmost respect for those being served, and being emphatic in doing so. Accordingly, Sheikh Al-Ḥakīm al-Tirmidhī stated that two of the conditions of service are humility and wilful surrender.[178] If the *fatā* finds himself feeling superior or looking down at others, he should immediately find a way to perform some sort of service for them to rid his heart of arrogance and self-satisfaction. Imam Jaʿfār al-Sādiq said that the people of service are those who seek to break their egos.[179]

THE PATH OF SACRED MANHOOD NECESSITATES SHOWING RESPECT TOWARDS ONE'S PARENTS & ELDERS.

Good Conduct
Towards Parents

One of the most vital duties of the *fatā* is to fulfil the rights due to his parents followed by his close kin, especially the elders among them. The path of sacred manhood necessitates showing respect and kindness towards one's parents and elders. Allah ﷻ stated in *Surah al-Nisā'*, verse 36:

> *And worship Allah and associate none with Him. And have excellent behaviour towards your parents, close kin, orphans, the poor, near and distant neighbours, close friends, wayfarers, and bondspeople in your possession. Surely Allah does not love whoever is arrogant, boastful.*

Furthermore, Allah ﷻ said in the 23rd and 24th verses of *Surah al-Isrā*:

> *And your Lord has decreed that you do not worship any except Him, and to parents, excellent treatment. Whether one or both of them reach old age [while] with you, say not to them [so much as], 'Uff,' and do not repel them but speak to them a noble word. And lower to them the wing of humility out of mercy and say, 'My Lord, have mercy upon them as they brought me up [when I was] young.'*

Imam Zayd ibn ʿAlī said:

> And the right of Allah pertaining to good conduct towards one's parents is to treat them excellently and with kindness, for Allah knows that even if something as insignificant as 'Uff' is said, He has prohibited such words from being said to them.[180]

The Prophet was asked, 'Which deed is most beloved to Allah?' He replied, 'Prayer at its appointed time.' Then he was asked, 'Then what?' He replied, 'Then being good to parents.' Then he was asked, 'Then what?' He answered, 'Then struggling in the path of Allah.'[181]

Sayyid ʿAbd al-Qādir al-Jīlānī explained that *be good to his parents* means obeying them, preserving good comportment when living with them or keeping company with them, and taking care of their rights in the correct manner.[182] It is also reported that the Prophet stated, 'Being good to parents is more virtuous than prayer, fasting, Hajj, *ʿumrah,* and struggling in the path of Allah.'[183] Following this prophetic tradition, Imam ʿAlī ibn Abī Ṭālib said, 'Being good to parents is the greatest religious obligation.'[184]

When Fuḍayl ibn ʿIyāḍ was asked about what constitutes good conduct towards one's parents, he replied that is it not being too lazy to serve them.[185] In regard to the duties of showing love and keeping company with one's parents, the *fatā* is to prioritize his mother, in accordance to the statement of Allah in *Surah Luqmān,* verse 14:

> *And We have enjoined on man to be good to his parents. His mother bore him in weakness and hardship upon weakness and hardship, and his weaning is in two years give thanks to Me and to your parents, unto Me is the final destination.*

Reflecting on this verse, the Prophet famously said, 'Paradise is under the feet of mothers'.[186] In another tradition, Bahz ibn Ḥakīm narrated from his father who narrated from his grandfather, who

Surely Allah advises you regarding your mothers, then advises you regarding your mothers. Then He advises you regarding your fathers. Then He advises you regarding your close kin, and then your close kin.

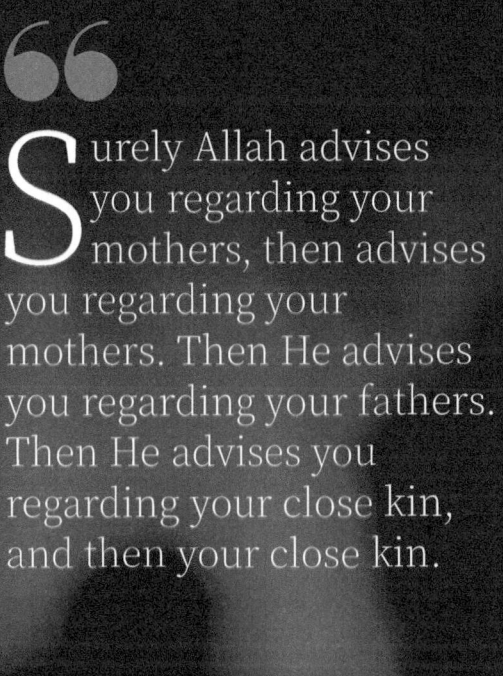

said: 'I asked, "O Messenger of Allah, who am I to be the kindest towards?" He replied, "Your mother." I asked, "Then who?" He said, "Your mother." I asked, "Then who?" He replied, "Your mother." I asked again, "Then who?" He then responded, "Your father."'[187]

Ibn 'Umar witnessed a Yemeni man making Tawaf around the House [the Kaaba] while carrying his mother on his back while saying, 'I am her humble camel. If her mount is scared, I am not scared' Then he asked, 'O Ibn 'Umar, do you think I have repaid her?' Ibn 'Umar said, 'No, not even for a single pang [of labour].'[188] Such is the exalted station of the mother in Islam, that it is reported that Zayn al-'Ābidīn said regarding the status of the mother:

> The right of your mother is that you know that she carried you where no one carries anyone, she fed you the fruit of her heart that no one gives to anyone, and she protected you with her all her organs. She did not care if she went hungry, if you could eat; if she was thirsty, as long as you drank; if she was naked, as long as you were clothed; if she was in the [heat of] the sun, as long as you were shaded. She gave up sleep for your sake; she protected you from heat and cold, all in order that you might belong to her. You will not be able to show her gratitude, unless through God's help and giving success.[189]

After the mother, the *fatā* is to prioritize his father whom his seed of life began. Moreover, the deference which the father is due is above all other living men, even if he is a disbeliever. Abū Hurayrah saw two men together, then he said to the younger one, 'Who is he to you?' The young man responded, 'My father'. He then told him, 'Do not address him by his first name, nor walk in front of him, nor sit down before him.'[190]

Zayn al-'Ābidīn reportedly said regarding the status of the father:

> The right of your father is that you know that he is your root, and you are his branch. Without him, you would not be. Whenever

> you see anything in yourself that pleases you, know that your father is the root of this blessing upon you. So, praise and thank Allah upon the measure of that – and there is no strength except by Allah.[191]

The Prophet ﷺ employed repetition to convey the importance of family, stating:

> Surely Allah advises you regarding your mothers, then advises you regarding your mothers. Then He advises you regarding your fathers. Then He advises you regarding your close kin, and then your close kin.[192]

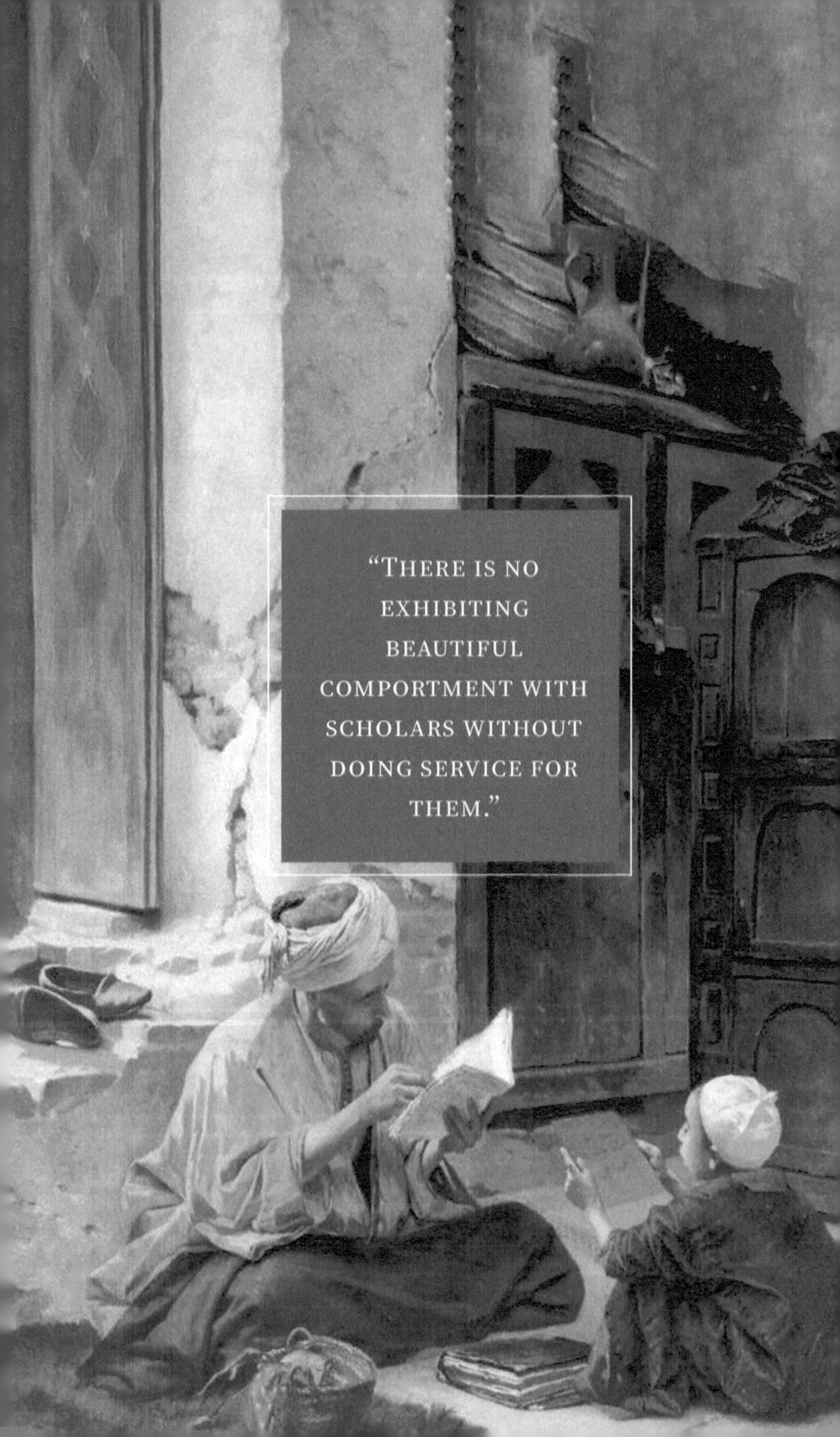

"There is no exhibiting beautiful comportment with scholars without doing service for them."

Deference Towards **Scholars and Spiritual Mentors**

Just as the *fatā* is to fulfil the rights of his parents and elders among his close kin, he has the duty to show deference and respect towards scholars and his spiritual mentors or guides, once such a guide has become apparent to him. This is especially needed today when religious authority is not only being minimized in general in the West, but also is being actively subverted - knowingly and unknowingly - by many Muslims themselves. This ranges from so-called reformists who claim that they can perform their own reinterpretations on issues about which there has been a sweeping consensus by scholars, to those who think that they can study books of hadith on their own and start giving their own religious decrees. This environment has led to the open disrespect of traditional scholars, causing many young Muslims to question the need for scholars or the conviction that young males need to humble themselves before spiritual mentors.

Allah ﷻ and His Messenger ﷺ mentioned the praiseworthy status of the scholars. He ﷻ said in *Surah Fāṭir*, verse 35, *'Of His servants, only the People of Knowledge are truly in awe of Allah. Surely Allah is the Almighty, All-Forgiving.'* In the 13th verse of in *Surah al-Naḥl*, Allah ﷻ also stated, *'So, ask the People of Remembrance if you do not know.'* Elaborating on this, the Prophet ﷺ said, 'Surely the scholars are the inheritors of the Prophets.'[193]

Allah ﷻ mentioned in His noble book the spiritual requirement for the sincere *fatā* to recognize the need for obtaining a guide and to then show deference to this man of experiential knowledge and wisdom. The indication of this is pointed to regarding the story of Mūsā ﷺ and his spiritual guide al-Khiḍr ﷺ. Allah ﷻ said in *Surah al-Kahf,* verses 65 and 66:

> *There they found a servant of Ours, to whom We had granted mercy from Us and taught with knowledge of Our own. Mūsā said to him, 'May I follow you, provided that you teach me what you have been taught of right guidance?'*

The deference which the *fatā* should have for the scholars as well as one's spiritual mentor or guide is a matter which has outward and inward aspects. Sayyid ʿAbd al-Salām al-Asmarī[r] said:

> You are obligated to have comportment with Allah, His Messenger, with your spiritual guides, and with all people, be the person pious or immoral. Comportment with spiritual guides is to protect their honour, have good conduct in serving them, and sincerity in loving them.[194]

Among the outward aspects, there are varying ways of honouring scholars and one's guide. The Prophet ﷺ stated, 'He is not of us who does not show mercy to the young and honour the elderly'.[195] The word 'elderly' can carry the meaning of one who is senior in knowledge, not just one who is an elder in age.

Just as the *fatā* is not to raise his voice at his parents, he should

r Sayyid ʿAbd al-Salām al-Asmarī was a 9th century AH Mālikī scholar and ascetic from Libya who was a descendant of Imam Idrīs ibn ʿAbdullāh ibn al-Ḥasan ibn al-Ḥasan ibn ʿAlī ibn Abī Ṭālib.

"You are obligated to have comportment with Allah, His Messenger, with your spiritual guides, and with all people, be the person pious or immoral. Comportment with spiritual guides is to protect their honour, have good conduct in serving them, and sincerity in loving them."

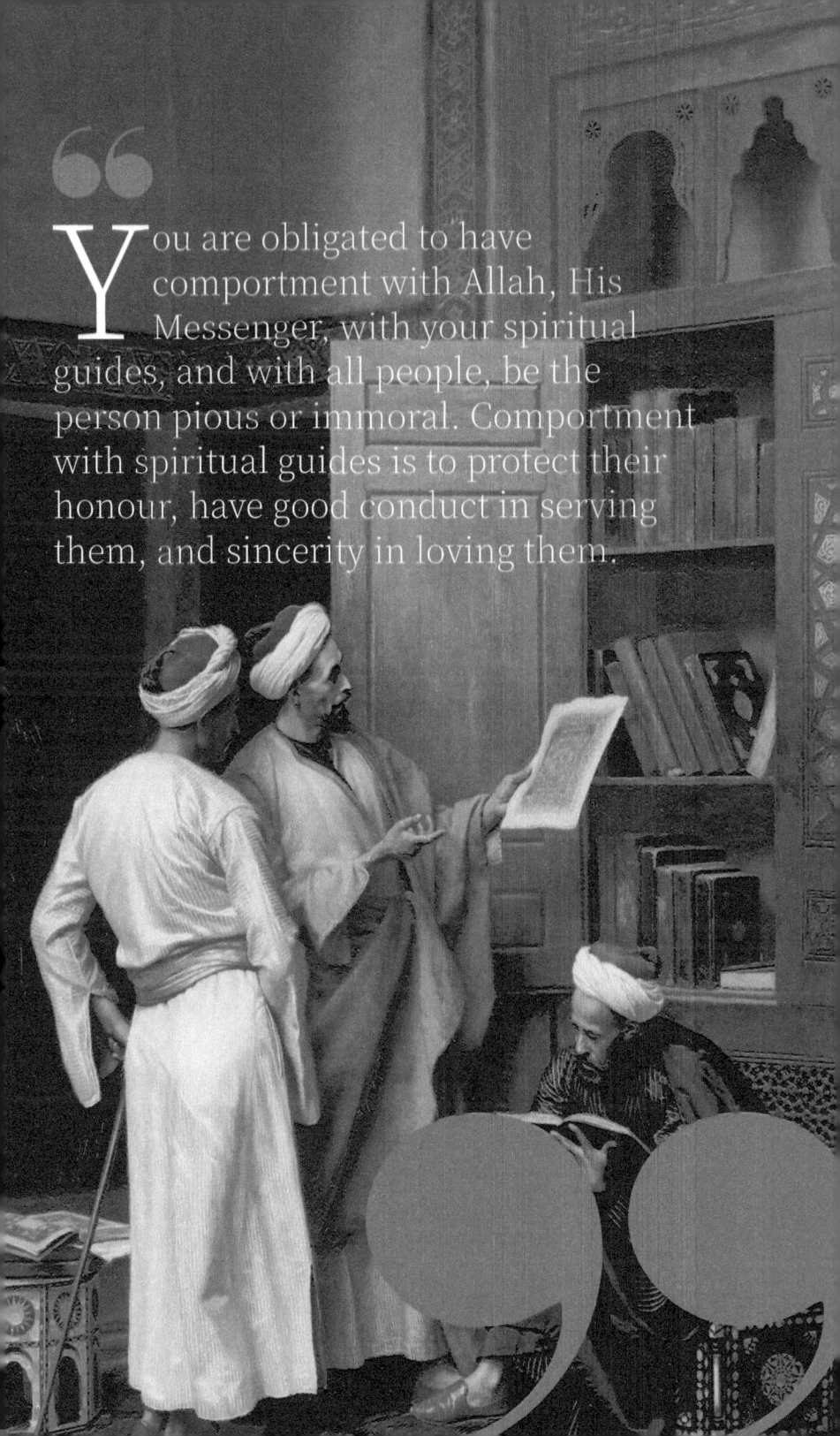

likewise not raise his voice at his spiritual mentor or guide. Just as one should not walk before their father (unless given permission, or for a specific reason such as to aid him or guard him against potential harm), Sayyid ʿAbd al-Qādir al-Jīlānī ؓ stated that one should not walk in front of their spiritual guide.[196] Sayyid al-Jīlānī also mentioned that one of the acts of humility to be shown to one's guide is to avoid turning one's physical back or backside to him.[197] Also when one's guide comes to an area in which the *fatā* is seated, he should stand up out of respect, as the Prophet ﷺ told the men of Banū Qurayẓah to stand for Saʿd ibn Muʿādh ؓ, saying 'Stand up for your master (*sayyid*)'.[198] Likewise, the *fatā* should not sit before their spiritual mentor or guide until he sits, unless given permission to do so.

Sayyid al-Jīlānī further mentioned that the *fatā* should not enter into a gathering or room in which one's guide is present without receiving permission.[199] After sitting in his company while he is instructing or speaking, the *fatā* should not talk to anyone, except to warn people of danger or to mitigate physical harm out of necessity. He should not pre-emptively answer a question directed to a scholar or spiritual guide, nor should anyone argue or debate in his gatherings, whether he is present or excuses himself. The *fatā* should not joke around or laugh loudly in his guide's gatherings; rather he should listen and be silent, unless he is asked a question by the scholar or guide, or is asked by the scholar to address the gathering from his generosity.

One of the outward displays of showing respect for scholars and one's guide is to kiss their foreheads or hands. Naturally, this only applies to male scholars, as it is completely improper for the *fatā* to kiss the hands of female scholars. It is narrated that when Jaʿfar ibn Abī Ṭālib ؓ returned from Abyssinia, he kissed the Messenger of Allah ﷺ on his forehead.[200] On another occasion when Anas was asked, 'Did you touch the Prophet ﷺ with your hand', he replied, 'Yes, I kissed it [his hand]'.[201] The Prophet ﷺ also reportedly stated, 'It is not permitted for anyone to kiss another hand [after myself] except for a man from the People of my Household or the hand of a scholar'.[202] Al-Suhrawardī stated, 'For the people of Islamic spirituality, kissing the hand of their guide after seeking forgiveness is a foundation of the Sunnah'.[203] In gatherings of students of knowledge, I have witnessed them kissing their teachers' hands. For instance, after a one-on-one gathering in which I read a text with our Sheikh Lo al-Mālikī, may Allah preserve him, from Touba, Senegal, I kissed his hand, he kissed mine in return, and then I kissed his hand again.

Among the inward aspects of deference towards scholars and one's spiritual mentor is loving them and having sincerity in all actions towards them. The *fatā* should pray that they are preserved and guarded from harm. Any service done for them should be for the sake of Allah ﷻ, which includes both good deeds they may be aware of as well as good deeds done for them without their knowledge. Sayyid 'Abd al-Qādir al-Jīlānī mentioned that 'there is no exhibiting beautiful comportment with scholars without doing service for them'.[204] Finally, the *fatā* should also not wish ill upon his teachers, nor should he ever wish for any favour of Allah to be stripped from them.

"Whoever is generous will be honoured, and whoever is stingy will be humiliated."

Generosity

According to Sayyid ʿAbd al-Qādir al-Jīlānī ﷺ, a foundational quality of the path is generosity, embodied by our Master Ibrāhīm ﷺ.[205] Being generous with a thing means giving of it to others.[206] The first level of generosity (*sakhāwah*) lies in the giver providing the petitioner or beggar with what he or she asks for.[207] Speaking about generosity, Allah ﷻ said in *Surah al-Ḥashr,* verse 9: *'And whoever is saved from the selfishness of their own souls, it is they who are successful.'* Regarding this, the Prophet ﷺ reportedly stated, 'Blessings concerning one's wealth are in giving zakat, commiserating with the believers, and keeping ties with close kin.'[208] He also advised us that 'the beggar has a right [to be given to] even if he comes to you riding a horse'[209] and reminded us that ' the generous ignoramus is more beloved to me than the stingy worshipper'.[210]

There are a number of other prophetic narrations on this topic: the Prophet ﷺ reportedly stated that 'the friend of Allah is formed upon generosity and beautiful character'.[211] Indeed, 'Paradise', as the hadith tells us, '...is the abode of the generous.'[212] Such is the lofty station of generosity that the Prophet ﷺ also said:

> The saints of my community will not enter paradise merely by deeds, but they will enter it by the mercy of Allah, the generosity of themselves, and by the soundness of their hearts.[213]

Jābir ibn ʿAbdullāh ﷺ said, 'It never happened that the Messenger of Allah ﷺ was asked for anything and said, "No"'.[214] ʿAlī ibn Abī Ṭālib, the Commander of the Faithful ﷺ, defined generosity as 'relinquishing indebtedness by giving',[215] also declaring that 'whoever gives with a short hand will be given by the Long Hand'.[216] The phrase 'long hand' is of course a metaphor, with the intended meaning of Allah ﷻ acting as the Giver – the phrase is not meant to be understood as a physical hand.

Sayyid ʿAbd al-Qādir al-Jīlānī reportedly explained that the context of revelation for verse 55 in *Surah al-Mā'idah* relates to Imam ʿAlī being in the position of Rukūʿ in prayer in al-Masjid al-Nabawī when a beggar called out in need. Hearing this, the Imam then stuck out his little finger that had a ring on it, intending for the beggar to take it as charity. After the beggar then took the ring off his finger, the Prophet ﷺ recited the verse relating to this event: *'Your protector is [naught] but Allah, His Messenger and those who believe, establish prayer, and give zakat – and they are those who bow down (make Rukūʿ in prayer).'*[217] Offering further commentary regarding generosity, Imam Jaʿfār al-Sādiq ﷺ said:

> Generosity is the character of the Prophets, and it is a pillar of the religion. One is not a believer except that he is generous, and no one is generous except a possessor of certitude and great determination. Generosity is a sign of the light of certainty; whoever knows the insignificance of their self will give something.[218]

It is said that Sufyān ibn ʿUyaynah was asked, 'What is generosity?' He replied, 'Good conduct with your brothers, and being generous with your wealth.'[219] Another scholar, Sheikh ʿAbdullāh ibn ʿAbbās al-Yāfaʿī, said, 'Complete generosity is to give your being for the sake of Allah, the Most High.'[220]

Following what was described above, the next rank of generosity (*jūd*) consists of giving without being asked or begged of.[221] The

Prophet ﷺ reportedly said, 'Surely Allah is Generous; He loves the generous. And He loves noble character, and He despises poor character.'[222] So too did Imam ʿAlī say that 'Generosity is from other than fear, and the deeper reality of generosity is in giving without hope of a reward'.[223] His son, Al-Ḥusayn ibn ʿAlī ﷺ said, 'Whoever is generous will be honoured, and whoever is stingy will be humiliated.'[224] Giving an example of this virtue in practice, Abū Hamzah al-Thumālī related:[225]

> Zayn al-ʿĀbidīn used to carry a sack of bread on his back during the night, and would dispense it [at poor families' homes]. While doing this, he would say, 'Surely giving charity in secret extinguishes the anger of the Lord ﷻ.'

ʿAmr ibn Dīnār conveyed a similar example of generosity:

> ʿAlī ibn al-Ḥusayn walked in on Muhammad ibn Usāmāh in Zayd when he was severely ill, whereupon he [Muhammad bin Usāmāh] began crying.
>
> ʿAlī ibn al-Ḥusayn asked, 'What's the matter?'
>
> Muhammad ibn Usāmāh replied, 'I have major debts that I owe.'
>
> ʿAlī ibn al-Ḥusayn inquired, 'How much is it?'
>
> Muhammad ibn Usāmāh said, '15,000 dinars.'
>
> ʿAlī ibn al-Ḥusayn told him, 'It is my debt now.'[226]

It has been related that Sheikh ʿAbd al-Qādir al-Jīlānī was generous with his wealth, giving it to the indigent, the poor, and orphans. He gave people food to eat and spent upon the needy in all times and occasions. He made food available for the elderly, and gathered the indigent and poor under his roof, sitting with them.[227] Enacting these two levels of generosity will lead to the next station of generosity, to be covered later in this book alongside the virtue of altruism.

"If you do not have shame, then do as you wish."

Modesty

One of the lost virtues of this era which the *fatā* must struggle to exemplify is modesty (*ḥayā*). The linguistic definition of modesty is being bashful and having decent conduct in front of others.[228] In its etymology, modesty is related to the word life (*hayā'*); hence, the life of the *fatā* must be established upon modesty. The light of faith is connected to modesty; as the Prophet ﷺ said, 'Modesty is from faith.'[229] Imam Abū Ḥāmid al-Ghazālī elaborated on the meaning of modesty for the *fatā* when he stated, 'It is the middle way in between brash shamelessness and soft effeminacy.'[230] Thus, the *fatā* in his mindfulness must avoid his heart being carefree, for a lack of care translates into shamelessness. On this, Imam Jaʿfār al-Sādiq said that lacking shame is at the heart of hypocrisy and dissension. At the same time, he must not be bashful to the degree that he cannot speak up or even utter non-confrontational statements, nor can his shyness lead to him being scared to be in the public space around others, as is characteristic of many contemporary 'momma's boys' who well-nigh act as if they are afraid of their own shadows.

A complete lack of modesty is a greater ailment, however, as Imam al-Ṣādiq stated, 'Whoever modesty has been withheld from will indulge in every form of mischief.'[231] This is because the One whom the *fatā* must be shy before is Allah ﷻ. Sheikh Abū Ṭālib al-Makkī mentioned this as the first and most important level of bashfulness when he said, 'Modesty before the Creator is faith', which means a lack of shame before Allah ﷻ entails a deficiency in faith.[232] Having no shame in the heart before Allah ﷻ is an inward trait that is outwardly displayed by vulgar miscreants and hooligans. Imam ʿAlī ibn Abī Ṭālib ؇ said, 'Shame before Allah, Glorified is He, guards from the punishment of the fire',[233] and 'Modesty before Allah obliterates many potential mistakes.'[234]

The *fatā* must also have bashfulness in front of people after prioritizing shame before his Creator. The Companion Abū Saʿīd described the Prophet ﷺ as more modest in front of people than a virgin girl with a veiled face.[235] Accordingly, the Prophet ﷺ said, 'If you do not have shame, then do as you wish.'[236] The person who has no shame will behave wildly in public, saying foul words without regard for others, dressing in ways that are inappropriate for the occasion.

Imam ʿAlī said, 'Whoever makes modesty his clothing, people will not see his faults.'[237] Expounding on this, he also stated, 'Modesty is handsome character' and 'Shame is the key to goodness.'[238] Thus, when it comes to modest dress, the *fatā* – at the bare minimum – should cover his body with loose-fitting clothing from the top of his navel to the point below his knees, as this meets the obligatory requirements according to Islamic jurisprudence. However, his dress should also be appropriate for each time and location in which he is present. For instance, he should not go in front of young ladies in public wearing tank tops or t-shirts, even if the minimum *fiqhī* requirements are being met, as he should guard his own ego, being scrupulous so to avoid attracting undue attention to himself or arousing desire in them. This example combines the matters addressed in two statements by Imam ʿAlī when he said, 'The modesty of a man from his own ego is the fruit of faith' and 'Shame is the consort of chastity.'[239]

When the *fatā* is around other males who openly disclose their attraction towards the same gender or act openly effeminate, he should dress and behave with the same caution before them as he would before young ladies. When possible, he should avoid being in their presence altogether to avoid fitnah, staying away as a precaution against arousing forbidden desires, as part of modesty not to incite what is forbidden or invite others to engage in it.

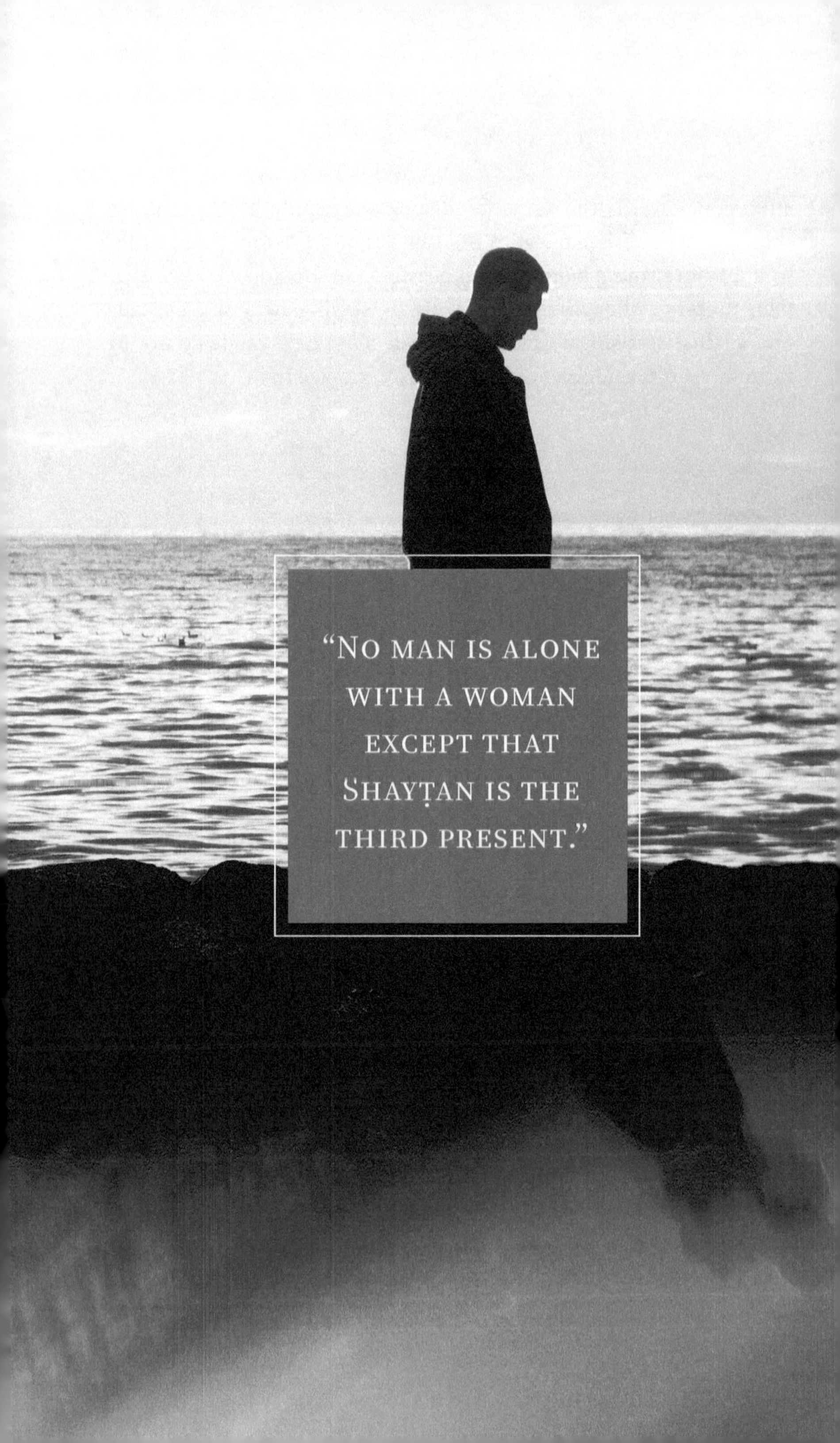
"No man is alone with a woman except that Shayṭan is the third present."

Restraining **Sexual Desires**

The *fatā* entering upon the path must also be vigilant in restraining his desires, for his four enemies are his ego, his desires, Shayṭān, and the world. His daily struggle (*jihād*) against his sexual desires is the greatest of struggles, often requiring more discipline than that of soldiers standing in straight ranks, following the commands of their commander. In *Surah al-Ḥajj,* verse 78, Allah ﷻ commands this struggle, saying, *'And struggle for Allah as is His due.'* Ibn al-Mubārak commented on this verse, explaining that it means 'the struggle against the self and desires.'[240] Additionally, al-Rāghib al-Iṣfahānī رحمه الله said that desire (*shahwah*), which is not inherently vain, is the longing of the self towards what it seeks.[241]

To reiterate, the greatest of the desires that the *fatā* must struggle to restrain is his sexual desires. This has become an even greater struggle for our generation compared to the generations of our pious predecessors, as societies in the West are much more overtly sexualized in uncountable ways. Grappling with such desires is not new, however, as described in *Surah Āl 'Imrān,* verse 14:

> *Alluring to men is the love of desires for women, [having] children, vast amounts of gold and silver, fine horses, cattle, and fertile land. These are pleasures of the worldly life, but Allah with Him is the best destination.*

Women are mentioned first among the creations desired by men. Sheikh Aḥmad Dem[s] said regarding this test:[242]

> [Women] are the most imminent allurement of the world…And [the Prophet] ﷺ said, 'There is not a test that comes upon men that brings more harm than women.'

The *fatā's* desire for women must be diverted from blameworthy sexual activity and guided towards fulling it in a manner that conforms with the sacred law. Such blameworthy activities include engaging in fornication and fellatio with women who are not wives. Acceptable wives are women who are permissible to marry according to the sacred law, to the exclusion of polytheists. Moreover, the *fatā* is prohibited from masturbating, whether he is doing so while fantasizing about women or looking at pornography – pornography, as a category, is prohibited in and of itself.

Sheikh Dem mentioned that some of the people of wisdom from the past said:[243]

> Allah created the angels with intellect without desire. Animals possess desires without intellect. However, man was created with both [desire and intellect]. So, whoever uses their intellect to conquer his desire is better than the angels, but whoever allows his desire to defeat his intellect is lower than animals.

The *fatā* has no authority to dictate to others how they ought to gather in society, nor does he have the authority to demand how women dress in public. He has the responsibility, however, to take precautionary steps and react, when necessary, to protect himself from falling into blameworthy sexual conduct, as his sexual desires are the strongest from when he reaches the age of puberty up until

---

s Sheikh Aḥmad Dem bin Muhammad al-Amin Bar Dem was a 20th century Fulani scholar from Sokone, Senegal that mastered Mālikī fiqh, the sciences of Tafsīr, and spirituality.

he becomes more physically mature in his mid-thirties.

The *fatā* should regularly supplicate for protection from sexual immorality, patience, and perseverance, turning to Allah ﷻ for divine support in his struggle. When he has urges arising from his attraction for women, he should immediately seek refuge with Allah ﷻ from Shayṭān, as his whispers incite him to act upon what is forbidden. He should also make a habit of waking up from his sleep in the last third of the night to pray *tahajjud*, seeking Divine assistance.

The Prophet ﷺ said, 'Fasting is a shield.'[244] Fasting is a shield from the corruptions of the world and is a barrier from the punishment of the Hereafter. For everything is a gate, and the gate of worship is fasting.[245] The *fatā* should also make it part of his spiritual routine to fast a minimum of three days every month outside of the month of Ramadan. He should fast the illuminated days (13th, 14th, and 15th) every month. If his desires are still strong, he should fast these days along with every Monday and Thursday, which are days that the Prophet ﷺ used to fast. The linguistic meaning of fasting is restraint, and fasting helps in restraining behaviours and quieting desires.[246] The Prophet ﷺ said:

> O young people! Whoever among you can marry, should marry, because it helps him lower his gaze and guard his private parts, and whoever is not able to marry, should fast, as fasting diminishes his sexual power.[247]

The *fatā's* fasting, if sincere, will bring him to the true fast which Sayyid ʿAbd al-Qādir al-Jīlānī ﷻ said 'is restraint of the spiritual heart from making equals with Allah Most High, and restraint of the innermost self (*sirr*) from his love is a spiritual witness (*mushāhadah*) of none other than Allah Most High'.[248]

Along with fasting, the *fatā* should control his eating habits outside of fasting hours, as doing so when he is not fasting will also assist him in taming his sexual desires. One of the steps of the spiritual path of the seeker according to Sheikh 'Uthmān ibn Fūdī[t] is to be hungry, not eating except in accordance with one's necessary measure.[249] Being in a state of slight hunger is the opposite of being full, and eating until one is stuffed is physically and spiritually unhealthy. The Prophet said, 'The believer eats with one intestine[250] while the disbeliever eats with seven intestines.' The *fatā* should also avoid regularly eating red meat, especially beef, as consistent consumption of it can increase desires within him.

Allah offers advice on this topic in the 30th verse of *Surah al-Nūr*: *'Say [O Prophet] to the believing men to lower their gazes and protect their private parts. That is purer for them. Surely Allah is well-aware of what they do.'* Commenting on this, Imam Ja'fār al-Sādiq stated that lowering the gaze concerns anyone or anything that is forbidden.[251] Sheikh Aḥmadou Bamba[u] (may Allah sanctify his spirit) said that, in relation to this verse[252], 'The eye should not gaze to a thing that is forbidden. Of course not, the gaze should be lowered away from it being respectful.'

It is narrated by 'Abdullāh ibn 'Abbās that his brother al-Faḍl ibn 'Abbās rode behind the Prophet on the back portion of his she-camel on the Day of al-Naḥr (the 10th of Dhū al-Ḥijjah during Hajj), and al-Faḍl was a handsome young man. The Prophet stopped to give the people verdicts. In the meantime, a beautiful young lady from the tribe of Kath'am came, asking a verdict of Allah's Messenger. Al-Faḍl started looking at her, as her beauty astounded him. The Prophet looked behind while al-Faḍl was looking at her, so the

---

t Sheikh 'Uthmān Ibn Fūdīo, otherwise known as Sheikh 'Uthmān dan Fodio was a Mālikī scholar of Fulani origin that lived between the late 18th century into the early 19th century. He established the Sokoto caliphate in what is today Northern Nigeria. His mother was a descendant of Prophet Muhammad.

u Sheikh Aḥmadou Bamba was a Senegalese Mālikī scholar who lived from the late 19th century to the early 20th century. He is the most prolific African scholar in writing poetry praising the Prophet Muhammad. His mother was a descendant of the Prophet as well.

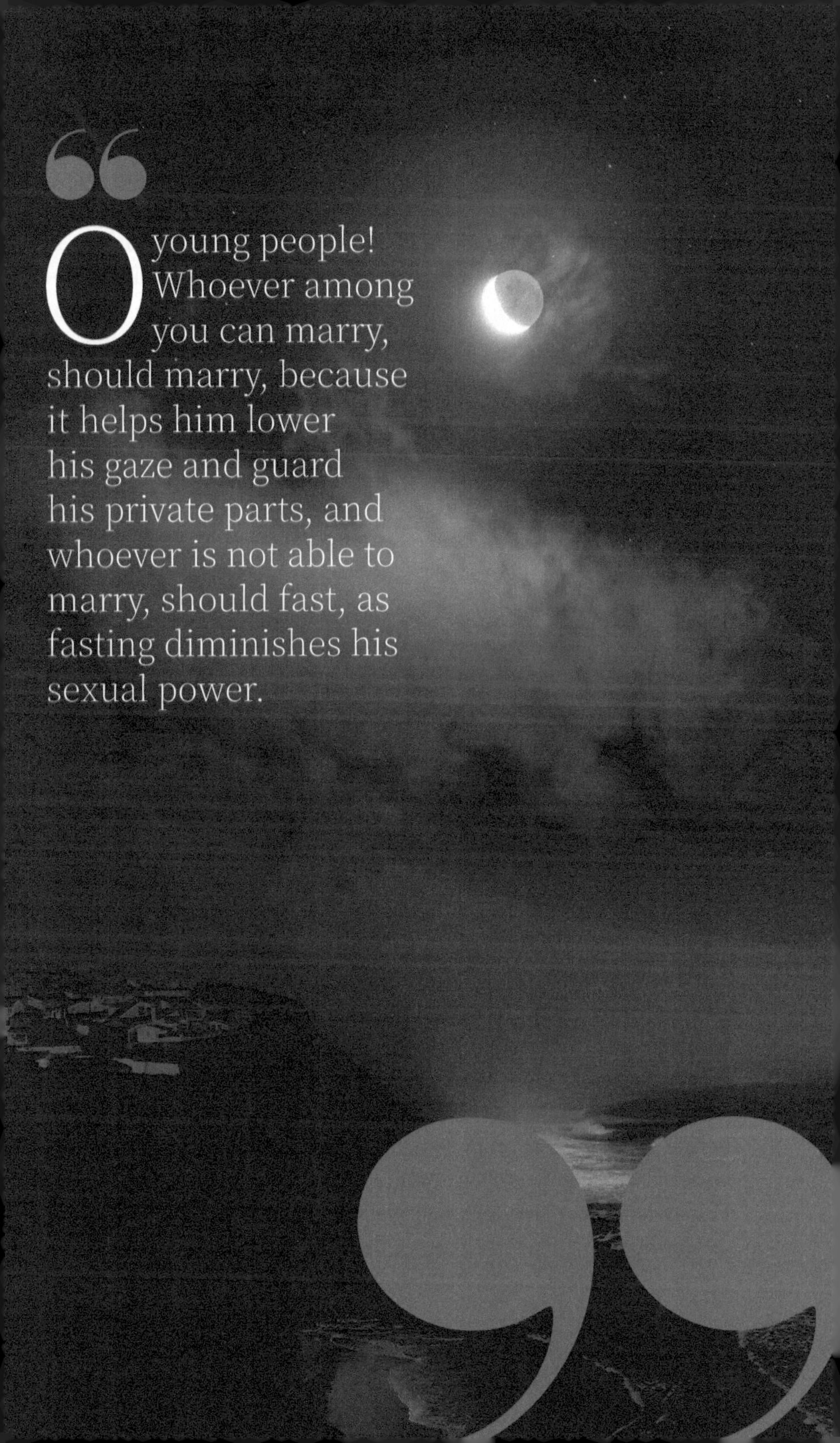

“O young people! Whoever among you can marry, should marry, because it helps him lower his gaze and guard his private parts, and whoever is not able to marry, should fast, as fasting diminishes his sexual power.”

Prophet held out his hand backwards and caught the chin of al-Faḍl, turning his face (so he could not gaze at her). She said, 'O Allah's Messenger! The obligation of performing Hajj enjoined by Allah on His worshipers has become compulsory on my father who is an old man and who cannot sit firmly on the riding animal. Will it be sufficient that I perform Hajj on his behalf?' He replied, 'Yes.'[253]

The Prophet ﷺ did not shun the young lady from asking the question, nor did he instruct her to use her hand to cover up the beauty of her face from al-Faḍl. Instead, he taught his younger cousin the importance of lowering his gaze by literally turning his face away from her. This story should serve as a reminder for the *fatā* to lower his gaze and guard his chastity, as the eyes are gateways to the soul.

The *fatā* must also guard his ears, which are likewise gateways to the soul and can incite passions. He is to refrain from listening to music that explicitly and implicitly has lyrics pertaining to sexual content. Much of today's music in the West, especially rap music, references sex at a purely animalistic level. I heard Imam Warith Din Mohammed say that such music reduces people to acting like dogs, dogs being shameless animals who publicly copulate with other dogs in front of people, unlike cats, who do not do so. The *fatā* should also avoid unnecessary phone conversations with women whose voices could arouse his desires. It is up to him to guard his own soul, not to blame women for who they are or how they sound.

The *fatā* is also obliged to completely avoid compromising situations with women who are not his wives that are lawful for him in marriage. The Prophet ﷺ said, 'No man should be alone with a woman except a close family member who is unlawful for him in marriage.'[254] He also warned the believers, saying 'No man is alone with a woman except that Shayṭān is the third present.'[255] Even if a woman has a young child present, the *fatā* should still not be behind closed doors with her, although they technically are not alone. Allah ﷻ conveyed the dangers of seclusion in *Surah Yūsuf*, verses 23-27:

And the lady, in whose house he lived, tried to seduce him. She locked the doors firmly and said, 'Come to me!' He replied, 'Allah is my refuge! It is not right to betray my master, who has taken good care of me. Indeed, the wrongdoers never succeed.'

She advanced towards him, and he would have done likewise, had he not seen a sign from his Lord; this is how We kept evil and indecency away from him, for he was truly one of Our chosen servants.

They raced for the door and she tore his shirt from the back, only to find her husband at the door. She cried, 'What is the penalty for someone who tried to violate your wife, except imprisonment or a painful punishment?'

Yūsuf responded, 'It was she who tried to seduce me.' And a witness from her own family testified: 'If his shirt is torn from the front, then she has told the truth and he is a liar.

But if it is torn from the back, then she lied while he is from the truthful.'

"COURAGE IS ONE OF THE TWO COMPONENTS OF HONOUR."

Courage

Courage is a noble trait which is to be embodied by the *fatā.* A linguistic definition of courage is that it is possessed by a real man is in his heart, displayed in his ease in going to battle and in his daring and fearless behaviour.[256] Al-Ghazālī ﷺ stated that courage 'is a characteristic [positioned] between being reckless and cowardly.'[257] The courage of the *fatā* is not foolhardy, like those who do not weigh the consequences of their actions, nor make proper preparations when entering into situations with potential danger; rather, courage means not being scared of any confrontation that has a righteous aim, although it may place him in front of potential harm, physically, materially, or reputationally. The virtue of courage in the *fatā* is the wedding of his righteous indignation when seeing a threat or looming injustice, and his hope in Allah ﷻ regarding outcomes.

The trait of courage is one of the three stellar characteristics which Anas ibn Mālik, who served the Prophet ﷺ described him to have after his passing – 'The Messenger of Allah was the most courageous of men.'[258] Speaking of past prophets, Allah ﷻ said in *Surah al-Baqarah,* Verse 251:

> *And thereupon, by Allah's leave, they routed them. And Dāwūd slew Jālūt; and Allah bestowed upon him dominion, and wisdom, and imparted to him the knowledge of whatever He willed.*

Ibn Kathīr said regarding this verse that it is an indication of the courage of Dāwūd ﷺ.[259] Dāwūd, though he was the youngest of his father's sons, showed great courage in battle. When Jālūt challenged men from the army of Ṭālūt to step forward to fight him, Dāwūd, who was a *fatā in the army,* confronted Jālūt. Jālūt, seeing him as a young boy, reportedly said to him, 'Go back, for surely I would hate to kill you.' Dāwūd replied, 'But I would love to kill you.' He then proceeded to pick up three stones, load one in his sling, and struck Jālūt, splitting his head asunder.[260]

Sayyid ʿAbd al-Qādir al-Jīlānī ﷺ and Sayyid ʿAbd al-ʿAzīz al-Dabbāgh both stated that the characteristic of courage was inherited by Imam ʿAlī ﷺ from the Prophet ﷺ.[261] The name 'Lion of Allah, the Victorious' was bestowed upon him for his valour, as being a lion is symbolic of being fiercely courageous.[262] This attribute coincides with the name Ḥaydar, also meaning lion, which was reportedly given to him by his mother Fāṭimah bint Asad ﷺ.[263]

Imam ʿAlī accompanied the Prophet ﷺ to every military campaign except for the Battle of Tabūk. He was on the frontline at the great Battle of Badr. He vanquished ʿAmr ibn ʿAbd al-Wudd, the champion of the pagan Arabs, at the Battle of Khandaq; his words with Ibn ʿAbd al-Wudd mirrored the brave speech of Dāwūd when he defeated Jālūt. He was the hero of the Battle of Khaybar, and when the battle standard was given to him, the Prophet ﷺ said 'that Allah will grant victory to a man who loves Allah and His Messenger, and whom Allah and His Messenger love.'[264] Regarding the Battle of Tabūk, which was before the Battle of Khaybar, the Prophet ﷺ specifically directed him to stay in Madinah, telling him 'Do you not want to be to me as Hārūn was to Mūsā, except there is no Prophet after me?'[265] His absence at Tabūk was not due to an unwillingness to confront the outward enemy, but due to obedience. During his time as Caliph, Imam ʿAlī later said to his Companions, 'O people! Surely if you do not fight, you will still eventually die. By He who possesses the soul of the son of Abū Ṭālib in his hand, a thousand blows with a sword upon the head is easier than death while under the covers in bed.'[266] He later achieved martyrdom when he was stabbed in the back by an accursed extremist armed with a poison-tip weapon while praying Fajr in Masjid al-Kūfah on the twenty-first of the blessed month of Ramadan.

Imam al-Ḥusayn ﷺ inherited the spiritual trait of courage from his father Imam ʿAlī. He accompanied his father into battles and followed him in peace. He likewise remained patient when his brother, Imam al-Ḥasan ﷺ, abdicated his position in governance to establish peace between two groups of Muslims. Imam al-Ḥusayn[267] also stated:

> Surely, I hope that Allah will give my brother reward based upon his intention concerning his love for restraint, and that He will reward me based on my intention concerning my love to struggle against oppressors.

When Yazīd, who was known for his vile behaviour and immorality, sat on the throne after the death of his father, Imam al-Ḥusayn courageously resisted pledging allegiance to him out of principle, giving up material wealth and endangering his life in the process. When advising his brother Muhammad ibn al-Ḥanafiyyah ﷺ before leaving Madinah, he wrote:

> Surely, I do not resist to cause mischief, nor due to reckless disregard, nor to commit corruption and wrongdoing. I resist only seeking reform within the Ummah of my grandfather Muhammad ﷺ, desiring to enjoin good and forbid evil and to follow the way of my grandfather Muhammad and my father ʿAlī ibn Abī Ṭālib.[268]

And he later preached in a sermon in Iraq:[269]

> Surely, you see truth but do not act in accordance with it yet see falsehood but do not prohibit yourselves from it. Certainly, the believer desires to return to Allah in a state of correctness. Surely,

I do not see death except as martyrdom, nor do I see life with oppressors except as dissatisfaction.

When Shimr ibn Dhī al-Jawshan al-ʿĀmirī, the killer of Imam al-Ḥusayn, threatened Zuhayr ibn al-Qays 🙏, a companion of Imam al-Ḥusayn, he replied to him, saying 'Are you trying to scare me with death? I swear by Allah that death with him [Imam al-Ḥusayn] is more beloved to me than living for eternity with you.'[270]

Imam al-Ḥusayn, along with his sons save for one, were martyred at Karbala on the tenth of Muḥarram known as the Day of Ashura, an occasion which is well-known. As for those who stated that it is inappropriate or a blameworthy innovation to fast on Ashura as it distracts from his martyrdom, Sayyid ʿAbd al-Qādir al-Jīlānī 🙏 answered[271]:

> Allah Most High, chose the grandson of His Prophet Muhammad 🙏 for martyrdom in the most noble and mighty of days and occasions and elevated him in it. Certainly, He increased him with that in his elevation in ranks and levels of nobility.

His one valiant son who survived, Ali Zayn al-ʿĀbidīn 🙏, was too sick to defend his father on Ashura, and his enemies found him to be so unwell that they incorrectly presumed that he would die.[272] He later regained his strength and courageously challenged Yazīd in the ruler's assembly in Damascus, during which his father's decapitated head was displayed nearby. He too would later achieve martyrdom after being poisoned by his adversaries.[273]

Imam Zayd inherited the spiritual quality of courage from his father Zayn al-ʿĀbidīn. He resisted the tyrannical rule of Hishām ibn ʿAbd al-Mālik. He declared, to the shock of Hishām's royal court, 'Whoever loves most the life of this world shall live humiliated.'[274] He was given moral and financial support by Abū Ḥanīfah 🙏, but eventually achieved martyrdom just as his forefathers had.[275] Abū Ḥanīfah himself later achieved martyrdom in prison due to persecution.[276] These acts of courage are but a few examples of the spiritual transmission of courage and investiture passed down through Imam ʿAlī.

From the explanations of courage, Imam ʿAlī stated, 'Courage is one of the two components of honour',[277] and, on another occasion, added that 'courage is an adornment' and 'the courage of a man is upon the measure of his pride'.[278] The great scholar Sheikh ʿUmar al-Suhrawardī also said, 'Courage is mediating indignation.'[279]

In this era, the *fatā* in the West does not display courage by rushing to a battlefield in a foreign land. The *fatā* is to be courageous in fulfilling his religious obligations for the sake of Allah ﷻ, knowing that there will be people who mock and harass him in an attempt to bully him into abandoning aspects of Islamic morality. His courage lies in being resolute in defending the safety of his family and property without depending on others to do so for him, abdicating his primary responsibility as a man. His valour is in his tenacity in defending the religion of Allah ﷻ in a dignified manner, neither going to the extreme of being harshly combative with those who insult his faith, nor being sheepish in the face of those who disparage or seek to intimidate his fellow Muslims. He is not masochistic or suicidal, and does not welcome being harmed, but will defend these sacred interests without warning if need be.

"SINCERE ADVICE IS FROM THE NOBLE TRAITS OF CHARACTER."

Sincere Advice

The *fatā*, in his concern for others, is at times obliged by his sense of justice to provide sincere advice (*naṣīḥah*) to both friends and adversaries. Linguistically, sincere counsel means to provide guidance towards what is upright and righteous, and to advise against what is corrupt and unrighteous.[280] Al-Qāshānī ؒ mentioned that sincere advice is the desire for good for people, making clear for them the path of righteousness and piety, aspiring to benefit them, and not desiring harm for them.[281] He mentioned this definition relating to sincere advice pertaining to what Allah ﷻ said regarding Hūd ؑ being sent to the People of ʿĀd, whereupon he said, 'I am conveying to you a message from my Lord, and I am for you a trustworthy advisor.' The sincere advice of a Prophet for his people was based on the absolute truth, not falsehood.

Imam al-Jazūlī stated that Prophet Muhammad ﷺ was the most praiseworthy of advisors as he was always sincere in his actions towards people and for the Creator.[282] Likewise, Imam ʿAlī ibn Abī Ṭālib ؓ said, 'Sincere advice is from the noble traits of character.'[283] These statements are a reflection of the prophetic statement that 'the religion is sincere advice'. Hearing this, the Companions said, 'To whom?', whereupon he replied, 'To Allah and His Book, to the Messenger, to the leaders of the Muslims, and to the common folk.'[284]

As the *fatā* should have protective jealousy to defend the Qur'an and the Prophet's honour, he may at times be placed in situations in which he must give advice to leaders or elders. His drive to do so should be due to his motivation for justice if he is put in an unavoidable position that such counsel must be given. He, however, should not blame nor approach someone as having committed injustice due to speculation out of ignorance. When Imam ʿAlī was asked which is better between generosity or justice, he replied, 'Justice is putting things in their proper places while generosity is extracting them away from their [original] destinations.'[285] Al-Qāshānī mentioned that Imam ʿAlī pointed towards justice being more virtuous than generosity because justice in governance is general, whereas generosity as demonstrated is specific; thus, justice is better and more virtuous of the two.[286]

When approaching leaders or elders to give advice in the immediate absence of one of their peers capable of doing so, the *fatā* should provide such counsel with kindness. And Allah, the Most High, said [in *Surah Tā-Hā*, verse 44] to Mūsā and his brother when He sent them to Firʿawn[287], *'So, speak to him gently in order that he remembers or fears [Allah].'*

People – including some ignorant elders – may attempt to appeal to the *fatā's* bravado by telling him to act from a position of rage and to forgo kindness when initially approaching one in a position of authority who is perceived to be unjust. The *fatā*, however, must struggle against this inclination to stay in accordance with the honourable code of conduct. It was the comportment of the righteous in the past to address rulers upon by their titles such as 'Commander of the Faithful' when advising them, even though many of them were involved in perpetrating injustice. Allah ﷻ said in *Surah Fuṣṣilāt,* verse 34, *'Not equal are good and evil, so repel evil with that which is better. Then, the one who is hostile towards you will be as a devoted, protecting friend.'* Warning against harshness, the Prophet ﷺ said, 'Whoever prohibits kindness has prohibited goodness.'[288] Imam ʿAlī also said,

“Not equal are good and evil, so repel evil with that which is better. Then, the one who is hostile towards you will be as a devoted, protecting friend.”

'The kindness of a person and his generosity may make him beloved to his adversaries.'[289]

The *fatā* is also supposed to give sincere advice to his friends and peers. Because of his closeness to them, he may see certain mistakes they have made that they cannot see in themselves. The Prophet ﷺ said regarding this that 'the believer is the mirror of the believer.'[290] Imam ʿAlī stated, 'The true friend is he who protects you, advises you regarding your faults, protects you in your absence, and gives to you over himself.'[291] He also said, 'Your friend prohibits you [from doing wrong] while your enemy is the one who instigates you.'[292] Just as the *fatā* gives advice, he must be willing to receive it as well. The spiritually immature and arrogant souls are those who can give advice, but are not willing to take it.

Allah ﷻ said in *Surah al-Balad,* Verse 17: *'Then he was of those who believe, enjoin upon each other steadfastness, and enjoin with compassion.'* Reflecting on this, the *fatā* should be compassionate in his counsel with his friends and peers, as this is from the spiritual disposition of the Prophet ﷺ as Allah ﷻ said of him in *Surah al-Tawbah,* verse 128, that he is *'with the believers very kind, very merciful'.* The Prophet ﷺ stated that, in general, 'Allah will not be merciful to whoever is not compassionate with people.'[293]

One of the aspects of the comportment of giving sincere advice is avoiding humiliating one's friends and peers in the process of advising them. Since the advice is being done out of love and wanting to see one's peers stay away from making mistakes that can harm themselves and others, the *fatā* should give his advice in private and not in front of others. It has reached us that the Prophet ﷺ allegedly said, 'Whoever advises his brother in public most certainly shames him.'[294] Similarly, it has reached us from our pious predecessors that the one who advises his friend in private beautifies him, while the one who advises him in public disgraces him. Loving counsel in private will more likely help those being advised and earn their endearment.

The *fatā* should know that his sincere advice may be met with dismissal or even hostility. He should remind himself before giving advice that Allah ﷻ is the final determiner of outcomes, and that the acceptance of his advice is not ultimately in his control. Also, what may appear to be the immediate dismissal of advice could perhaps be accepted later. If the one who has been given advice becomes hostile, Allah ﷻ instructed us, in *Surah al-Aʿrāf*, verse 199, to *'take to pardoning, enjoin good, and disengage with the ignorant.'*

When the reaction becomes hostile to the point of the *fatā* is being cursed out or is faced with a potential physical confrontation, it is more chivalrous to disengage rather than engage in an angry argument. This is from the wisdom of the saying that one should not argue with a loud fool, for surely people may err in distinguishing between the two. In many instances, the one who gives advice yet does not disengage when such situations arise will inevitably be defeated by the ignorance of the hostile person, as he lowers himself in behaviour by responding to ignorance with ignorant behaviour or speech unbecoming of the *fatā*.

"There is no sin more harmful for you than to show contempt for your Muslim brother."

Brotherhood

There is no *futuwwah* without brotherhood. The *fatā,* in his growing maturity, must understand that his own personal spiritual growth and the increase of blessings has a relationship with his connection with the *fityān* and the Muslim community in general. While linguists have said that brotherhood means brothers from the same lineage, brotherhood also encompasses brothers in friendship.[295] Regarding this, Allah ﷻ said in *Surah al-Ḥujurāt*, verse 10: *'The believers are but brothers, so reconcile between your brothers; and have mindfulness of Allah in order that you may receive [more of] His mercy.'* The Prophet ﷺ also said, 'From the joy of a person is that he has righteous, upright brothers.'[296] Likewise, Imam ʿAlī ibn Abī Ṭālib said that 'a righteous brother is better for you than yourself alone, for the ego commands [towards] evil while the righteous brother does not enjoin [anything] for you but good.'[297]

As Caliph, when Imam ʿAlī ibn Abī Ṭālib wrote to the governor of Egypt, Mālik al-Ashtar , he advised him concerning the Egyptians, 'Surely there are two types: either a brother for you in religion, or an equal for you in humanity.'[298] Furthermore, Imam ʿAlī said, 'Many a brother was born from other than your mother.'[299] Thus, there is an exclusivity of spiritual brotherhood among believers in Islam based upon faith that transcends common humanity and blood ties. This principle is firmly established in the following prophetic tradition:

> Do not hate each other, do not envy each other, do not turn away from each other, but rather be servants of Allah as brothers. It is not lawful for a Muslim to boycott his brother for more than three days.[300]

Sheikh 'Uthmān ibn Fūdī ﷺ stated:

> Surely spiritual allegiance for believers is a religious obligation upon every Muslim according to the Book [the Qur'an], Sunnah, and the consensus [of the scholars and righteous persons among the community].[301]

True brotherhood must consist of loyalty. A sign of the *fatā*'s sincerity for Allah ﷻ is that he does not break his oaths and agreements with his brothers when they conform with the Qur'an, Sunnah, and what is known to be good. The *fatā* should see his word as his bond that he will not break for anyone, for doing so would make him worse in character than a mangy, wild dog. Abū Bakr Muhammad ibn Khalaf ibn al-Marzubānī ﷺ highlighted in his book *The Merit of Dogs Over Many Who Wear Clothing,* that loyal dogs have a trait that many adult males lack.

This is illustrated in a story in which Ibn 'Umar ﷺ saw a Bedouin with a dog, then asked him, 'What is this with you?' The Bedouin replied, 'One who thanks me and keeps my secret.' Ibn 'Umar then responded, 'Then preserve your companion.'

Al-Sha'bī similarly said, 'The best quality of a dog is that he does not have hypocrisy in his love.' Ibn 'Abbās ﷺ added that 'a trustworthy dog is better than a treacherous man'.

The *fatā* should stand by his brothers in times of distress, just as a dog does not abandon his master when distress or danger comes to him. This was the that manifested between the emigrants and the helpers in Madinah when the Prophet ﷺ established the Brotherhood Compact (*mu'ākhāt*) between them. Encouraging this spirit of brotherhood, the Prophet ﷺ said:

> Whoever relieves the hardship of a believer in this world, Allah will relieve his hardship on the Day of Resurrection. Whoever helps ease one in difficulty, Allah will make it easy for him in this world and in the Hereafter. Whoever conceals the faults of a Muslim, Allah will conceal his faults in this world and in the Hereafter. Allah helps the servant as long as he helps his brother.

Brothers come to the aid of other brothers and commiserate with them. The Prophet ﷺ, for instance, made Salmān al-Fārisī and Abū Dardā' brothers, and Salmān visited Abū Dardā'. Abū Dardā' made food for him, then told him, 'Eat, though I am fasting.' Salmān replied, 'I will eat if you eat with me', and then Abū Dardā' broke his fast.

Likewise, the brotherly love between Hudhayfah ibn al-Yamān ؓ and Salmān was as such that he would give him water to drink from his own cup while holding it in his hand.

A true brother does not seek to dishonour his brothers by revealing their failings or personal mistakes to the public, nor does a real brother use his brothers' mistakes as leverage over them. To do such would be a spiritual breach of brotherhood and would cause division within the brotherhood.

Accordingly, the Prophet ﷺ said, 'Reviling a Muslim is grave corruption, and killing him is disbelief.' Strengthening this point, Ja'far al-Khuldī said, '*futuwwah* is to debase the one's ego and to ennoble the sanctity of Muslims.'

The *fatā* must control his tongue and hands during times of disagreement with his brothers by refraining from cursing or fighting with his brothers in faith. If he is angered by certain words or actions committed, he should remove himself from the situation to calm down instead of acting from rage, which will ultimately bring about regret. He should not shun the brothers for more than three days without calling forth an elder to help mediate any disputes.

The *fatā* is forbidden to make fun of his fellow brothers by bullying them or calling them names, as Allah ﷻ prohibited this in *Surah al-Ḥujarāt,* verse 10, when he proclaimed:

> *O you who believe! Do not let some men ridicule other men. Perhaps they are better than those [ridiculing]. Nor let some women ridicule other women. Perhaps they may be better than them. Do not defame one another, nor call each other by [offensive] nicknames. How evil it is to act rebelliously after having faith! And whoever does not repent, it is they who are the wrongdoers.*

Sayyid Muʿīn al-Dīn Chishtī[v] said, 'There is no sin more harmful for you than to show contempt for your Muslim brother.'[302] Thus, blameworthy tribalism and racism are spiritually cancerous and are part of Shayṭān's scheme to bring enmity between brothers in faith. The *fatā* must be vigilant in not falling into such trappings and should sway others away from racism when it arises. Racism is antithetical to Islam, as the Prophet ﷺ clearly stated:

> O people! Surely your Lord is One. Surely there is no virtue of the Arab over the non-Arab, nor the non-Arab over the Arab. There is no virtue of the white over the Black, nor the Black over the white except in God-consciousness. Surely the most honourable of you with Allah are those of you who are most regardful.[303]

---

v Muʿīn al-Dīn Chishtī was an ascetic from the 12th and 13 centuries C.E. who was a paternal descendent of Imam al-Ḥusayn ibn ʿAlī and a maternal descendant of Imam al-Ḥasan ibn ʿAlī. He was born in Persia and eventually settled in India, wherein many came to Islam through his teachings.

In the Brotherhood Compact, the Prophet ﷺ paired off different men from different tribes and made them best friends. He also paired off non-Arabs with Arabs. It is narrated that on one occasion, two clients of the Prophet ﷺ who were both Muslims began reviling each other, one shouting 'O Abyssinian!' while the other yelled 'O Egyptian!' At this, the Prophet ﷺ told them, 'Stop saying this! Both of you men are from the People of Muhammad.'[304] On another occasion, a man questioned Salmān al-Fārisī ؓ regarding his lineage. He responded[305]:

> My honour, my religion, and my lineage are the dirt; I was created from the dirt, and to the dirt will I return. Then I will be resurrected and brought to the scale. If my scale is heavy [with faith and good deeds], then my lineage will be most honourable, and I will have honour with my Lord and will enter paradise. But if my scale is light, then my lineage will be shameful; I will be disgraced in front of my Lord, and then I will be punished unless forgiveness and mercy are granted for my sins.

One day, ʿAlī ibn al-Ḥusayn ؓ entered the masjid, came before the people, then sat in a study circle led by Zayd ibn Aslam. Nāfiʿ ibn Jubayr ibn Muṭʿim, who was Qurashī, said to ʿAlī ibn al-Ḥusayn, 'May Allah forgive you. You are the master of people, excel in all circles of the people of sacred knowledge, and are from Quraysh, yet you sit with this black slave.' ʿAlī ibn al-Ḥusayn replied, 'I merely sit with a man wherever I find benefit, and surely knowledge is found wherever it exists.'[306]

A similar event took place in which a black man came to Jaʿfar al-Ṣādiq ؓ appearing distraught. When the Imam inquired as to what was wrong, he said that a Nabaṭī[w] man sought to put me down. Imam

---

w Nabtiyyah is an area of Semitic language speakers who were not yet Arabized and is now in modern day Lebanon.

> O you who believe!
> Do not let some men
> ridicule other men.
> Perhaps they are better
> than those [ridiculing].
> Nor let some women
> ridicule other women.
> Perhaps they may
> be better than them.

Do not defame one another, nor call each other by [offensive] nicknames. How evil it is to act rebelliously after having faith! And whoever does not repent, it is they who are the wrongdoers.

al-Ṣādiq replied, 'The foundation of a man is his intellect, his true lineage is his religion, his honour is his regardfulness, and people descending from Adam are equal.'[307]

Classism is likewise a divide-and-conquer tactic employed by Shayṭān to suggest that one should not associate with his/her fellow brothers or even look down upon them. This takes many forms, stemming from factors such as how much perceived wealth one has or which neighbourhood he resides in. We can see how the Prophet ﷺ dealt with such issues when they arose in the narrative of the Sīrah.

After migrating from Makkah to Madinah, some of the Companions who had no wealth were essentially homeless, so they slept in a special location in al-Masjid al-Nabawī.[308] These Companions, who wore garments of wool, included Khabbāb ibn al-Aratt, Ṣuhayb al-Rūmī, Bilāl al-Ḥabashī, Abū Dharr, and Salmān al-Fārisī. One day, a group of Arabs who considered themselves aristocrats told the Prophet ﷺ that they would not sit and talk with him while he was in the company of these poor Companions. 'Uyaynah ibn Ḥiṣn reportedly said the following to the Prophet ﷺ before accepting Islam:

> Certainly, I find the odour of Salmān al-Fārisī offensive. Make a separate gathering for us with you, so we do not gather with him. Then make a gathering with them so that we do not have to join him.

The Prophet ﷺ recited *Surah al-Kahf,* verse 18, in which Allah ﷻ instructed him:

> *And keep yourself content with those who call upon their Lord in the morning and evening seeking His countenance. And do not turn your eyes away from them seeking the allurement of the worldly life. And do not obey one whose heart is heedless of our remembrance and follows his vain desires and whose affair is negligent.*

After reciting this verse, the Prophet ﷺ said, 'All praise belongs to Allah, who made in my Ummah one with whom I was commanded to stay patient and content within myself with him.' Just as he loved those deemed socially insignificant himself, he commanded his followers to do the same, as it is reported that the Prophet ﷺ told Abū Dharr, 'Love the poor, look towards those who you perceive to be beneath you but do not look towards those who you perceive to be above you.'[309]

And in another setting, he also instructed him to 'love the poor, and keep company with them.'[310] Given that Abū Dharr was once in extreme poverty, this is a lesson to the *fatā* whose family came from poor or meagre backgrounds that they should not become arrogant when circumstances change, instead giving thanks to Allah ﷻ for increasing them in material sustenance.

The *fatā* should also know that the people of the *qiblah* constitute a single Ummah, and thus he should avoid those who sow seeds of division among Muslims based upon their group affiliations and sectarian politics. Sectarianism, for Muslims in the West who are small minorities weakens them, which makes them more vulnerable to those in dominant cultures who seek to defame and mock the Prophet ﷺ, and strip Muslims of their religious rights. Given that the *fatā* is to have vigilant care for the religion and his fellow Muslims, his sense of protection for all Muslims should prevent him from taking scholarly differences of opinion or group affiliations as a means to increase the vulnerability of the community. This principle of unity is manifest in the Qur'an, wherein Allah ﷻ states in *Surah al-Anfāl*, verse 46, *'And obey Allah and His Messenger and do not quarrel for then you will be weak in hearts and your strength will depart but be patient; surely Allah is with the patient.'* Likewise, He said in *Surah Āl 'Imrān*, verse 103:

And hold firmly to the rope of Allah and do not be divided. Remem-

ber Allah's favour upon you when you were enemies, then He united your hearts, so you—by His grace—became brothers. And you were at the brink of a fiery pit and He saved you from it. Thus, Allah makes His clear to you His signs in order that rightly guided.

The *fatā* should furthermore avoid social media sectarian arguments, staying away from those who claim their group is the only group upon the truth, a widely circulated statement by online personalities and debaters in videos. Those who instigate such disputes are usually junior students of knowledge (at best) rather than scholars. He must not be fooled merely because these males have a degree of charisma and large online followings. Their videos should not even be shared, as it could spark unnecessary trials and drama within the brotherhood of Islam.

The worst of such sectarianism expresses itself when some declare their fellow people of the *qiblah* are disbelievers or deviants, which has historically led to Muslims fighting and killing each other. The Prophet ﷺ warned against this, stating, 'If a man says to his brother "O disbeliever", then certainly one of them is such [a disbeliever].'[311] This means that if a man calls another disbeliever while he is not, then the one who called him such a thing has spoken words of disbelief, which is a grave sin. Violence between Muslims is an enormity, as Allah ﷻ stated in *Surah al-Nisā'*, verse 93: *'And whoever kills a believer intentionally, his punishment is Hell; he shall abide in it forever, and Allah will send His wrath on him and curse him and prepare for him a tremendous chastisement.'* Thus, the *fatā* should never forget the prophetic statement that 'every Muslim – for his fellow Muslim – is sacred in his blood, his property and his honour'.[312]

Imam ʿAlī was martyred by a Muslim from a group of rebels known as the Khawārij, who habitually denounced their fellow Muslims as deviants and heathens. There was infighting among Muslims in the time of the Abbasids, which led to the Mongols overtaking Baghdad. The Ottomans were declared polytheists by a group of extremists that received help from the enemies of the religion, leading to bloodshed in the Hijaz. In recent times, the terrorist group Daesh did the same in Northern Iraq and Syria, shedding the blood of Muslims. It is not the place of the *fatā* to declare people of the *qiblah* as deviants, to then join those who seek to harm other humans including Muslims. He should pray for those whom he may disagree with and be patient with them for Allah's sake to maintain brotherly fraternity.

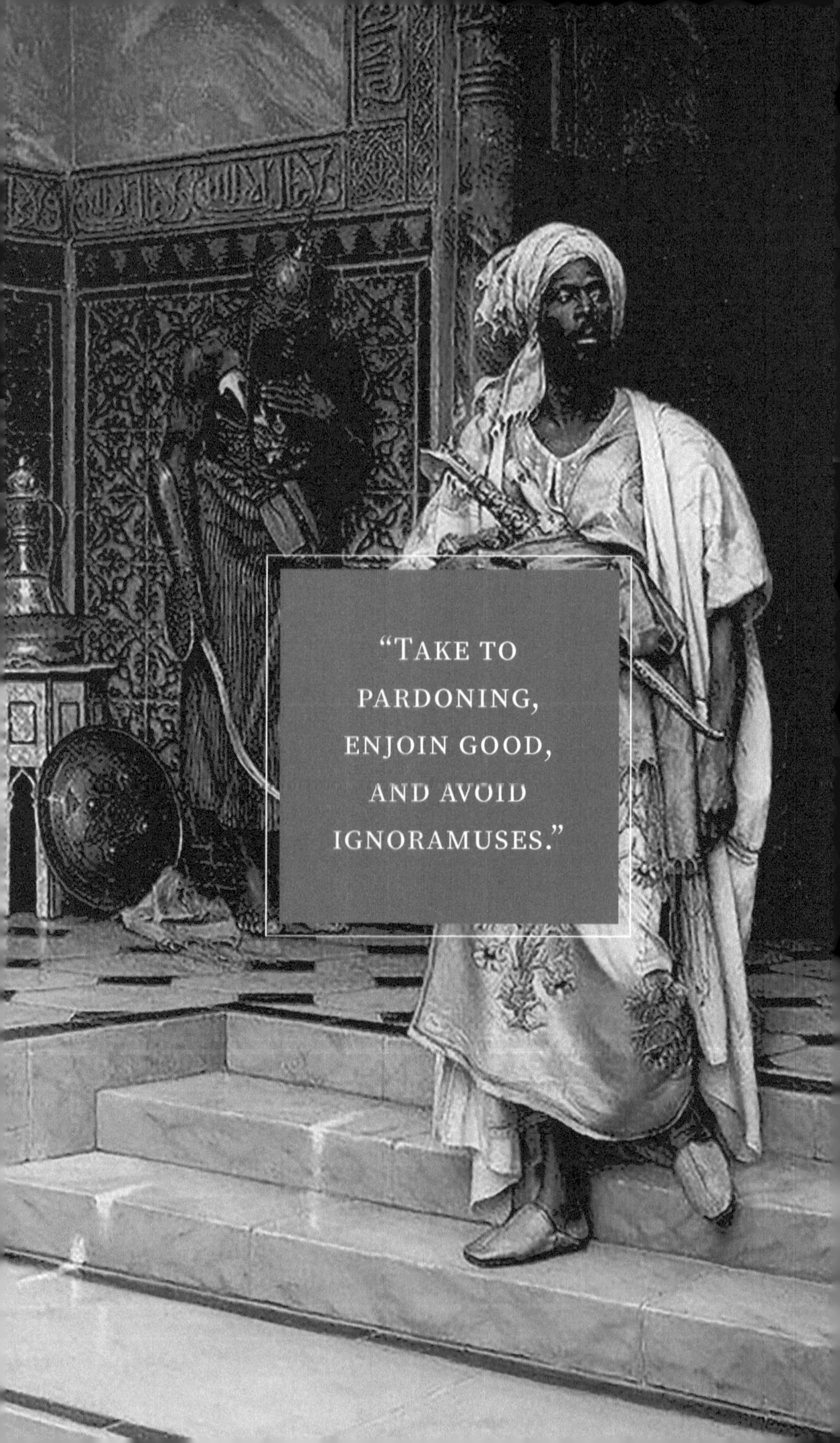

"TAKE TO PARDONING, ENJOIN GOOD, AND AVOID IGNORAMUSES."

Pardoning

One of the noble characteristics of *futuwwah* is the internal capacity to pardon others. Linguistically, one of the meanings of pardoning is to excuse a person without punishing him.³¹³ To pardon another is a virtue originating from the generosity of the *fatā*.³¹⁴ Pardoning brings ease to the self by abandoning the desire to punish the wrongdoer.³¹⁵ Imam Jaʿfar al-Sādiq said, 'Pardoning is to outwardly stick with your companion – though he did you wrong – and to inwardly forget the root of what he did that was wrong.'³¹⁶ To pardon someone is to forgive that person without bringing the matter up to them again as a type of leverage over them.

Imam ʿAlī ibn Abī Ṭālib, 'Pardoning is the most beautiful aspect of treating someone well', and 'pardoning is the crown of noble traits.'³¹⁷ Allah commanded the believers to do so in *Surah al-Aʿrāf*, verse 199: *'Take to pardoning, enjoin good, and avoid ignoramuses.'* It is narrated that when this was revealed, the Prophet said to the angel Jibrīl, 'What is this meaning, O Jibrīl?' He responded, 'Surely Allah has enjoined upon you that you pardon those who wrong you, give to those who restricted you, and reach out to those who cut you off.'³¹⁸

It is well-known that the Prophet pardoned and gave amnesty when he, along with his Companions, returned to Makkah after having witnessed some of his close Companions being tortured and killed by the leaders of Quraysh. Furthermore, his beloved wife Khadījah bint Khuwaylid ؓ died under an economic boycott, in which Muslims faced starvation and poverty at the hands of Quraysh. His Companions fled to Abyssinia and Madinah due to this persecution, and he, along with his close friend Abū Bakr ؓ, had to sneak out of Makkah facing threats to their lives. Nevertheless, those who perpetuated these crimes and were still living in Makkah were then pardoned by the Prophet of Mercy ﷺ. Allah ﷻ said in *Surah al-Zumar*, verse 53:

> Say, O My servants who have transgressed against their own souls, do not give up hope in the mercy of Allah. Surely, He can forgive you of your sins. He is the Oft-Forgiver, the Merciful Redeemer.

It was relayed that this verse relates to Waḥshī ibn Ḥarb, who killed the Prophet's uncle Ḥamzah ؓ at the Battle of Uhud.[319] The Prophet ﷺ pardoned him even though he killed his beloved uncle and mutilated his blessed corpse. Due to this, he reportedly said, 'There is not anything more beloved to me in the world and what is in it than this verse.'[320]

The Prophet ﷺ said, 'A servant does not pardon – seeking the countenance of Allah – wrong done to him except that Allah will elevate him by it.'[321] Reportedly Imam 'Alī once went to the Prophet ﷺ and said, 'Oh Messenger of God! A person came and killed my brother [in Islam]. I want retribution.' The Prophet responded, 'Retribution is prescribed for you in the matter of the murdered', quoting *Surah al-Baqarah*, verse 178, and said, 'This is God's command and the ruling of the Qur'an.' The Commander of the Faithful, 'Alī, replied, 'Oh Messenger of God! [Even] if I take retribution, my brother is still dead, is he not?' He replied, 'Yes, he is dead.' 'Alī said, 'Then I will not spill his blood, but I will bear this tyranny and pardon him. Is this permissible or not?' The Messenger ﷺ answered, 'May God bless you, those you love, and your children.'³²²

Speaking of the virtues of forgiveness, Allah ﷻ said in *Surah Āl 'Imrān*, Verse 134: *'Those who donate in prosperity and adversity, control their anger, and pardon others. And Allah loves the doers of good.'* Furthermore, it is reported that the Prophet ﷺ stated: 'A caller will proclaim on the Day of Resurrection, "Where are those who will receive their reward from Allah? Do not present yourselves except for those who pardoned others."'³²³

In another narration, 'Abd al-Razzāq reported that a female servant of 'Alī ibn al-Ḥusayn ؓ poured out some water as he prepared to pray, and she dropped the pitcher onto his head. The female servant then said, 'Surely Allah ﷻ says [in *Surah Āl 'Imrān,* verse 134]:

> *"Those who control their anger."'*
>
> He replied: 'I have restrained my anger.'
>
> She said: *'And those who pardon others.'*
>
> He replied: 'Allah has pardoned you.'
>
> She said: *'And Allah loves the doers of good.'*
>
> He said: 'Go, for you are now free.'³²⁴

"When you make soup, put more water in the broth, and take care of your neighbour."

Honouring
Neighbours and Guests

An aspect of the chivalry embodied by the *fatā* is honouring his neighbours and guests, irrespective of their religion. Linguistically, a neighbour means whoever adjoins or is in proximity to one's residence.[325] When Ḥasan al-Baṣrī ﷺ was asked who is considered a neighbour, he replied, 'forty homes in front, forty homes from behind, forty homes to the right, and forty homes to the left'.[326] In a fuller sense, neighbours means those who resides in one's village, neighbourhood, or local community.

Allah ﷻ mentioned the importance of the neighbour in *Surah al-Nisā',* verse, 36:

> *And worship Allah and do not associate anything with Him, be kind to your parents and your close kin, and to orphans, near and distant neighbours, close friends, the wayfarer, and those bondspeople in your possession. Surely Allah does not like whoever is arrogant, boastful.*

Likewise, the Prophet ﷺ said, 'Jibrīl kept advising me regarding the neighbour to the point that I thought they would be assigned inheritance.'[327] In a similar narration, Mujāhid ibn Jabr ﷺ said, 'I was with ʿAbdullāh ibn ʿAbbās ibn ʿAmr while his young servant was skinning a sheep. He said, "Boy, when you finish, start [sharing] with the Jewish neighbour." A man from his people then exclaimed, "Jewish?! May Allah correct you!" He replied, "I heard the Messenger of Allah ﷺ advise us to treat our neighbours well until we feared (or we thought) that he would order us to make them our heirs."'[328]

The *fatā*'s first responsibility towards his neighbours is not to harm them with either his hand or tongue. The Prophet ﷺ said, 'The Muslim is the one from whose tongue and hands the, people are safe, and the believer is the one from whom the people's lives and wealth are safe.'[329] He also stated, 'The final hour will not be established until a man kills his neighbour, brother, or father.'[330] Thus, the *fatā* should not be bothersome towards his neighbours, nor should he intrude into their personal business that goes on within their homes. Allah ﷻ said in *Surah al-Ḥujarāt,* verse 12:

> *O you who believe! Avoid much suspicion; indeed, some suspicion is sinful. And spy not, neither backbite one another. Would one of you like to eat the flesh of his dead brother? No, you would hate it. And be regardful of Allah. Surely, Allah is the Acceptor of Repentance, the Merciful Redeemer.*

Regarding this, the Prophet ﷺ said, 'Protect yourselves from people who harbour blameworthy suspicion.'[331] Al-Tustarī mentioned that the command not to spy on others means to not investigate their faults which Allah ﷻ has covered.[332] This is the prophetic practice, as the Prophet ﷺ said, 'From the beauty of a person's Islam is leaving along what does not concern him',[333] and likewise, it is reported that ʿĪsā ﷺ said, 'Do not look into the sins of people like you are lords.'[334]

The Prophet ﷺ said, 'He is not a believer who is full while his neighbour is hungry.' This statement should signal to the *fatā* that he should know his neighbours and converse with them, as he cannot know if his neighbours are hungry without establishing friendly relations with them first. He should willingly share his food with his neighbours suffering from hunger, just as the Prophet ﷺ instructed Abū Dharr ؓ, 'When you make soup, put more water in the broth, and take care of your neighbours.'[335] It is well-known that 'Alī ibn al-Ḥusayn ؓ would secretly leave bread at night for his neighbours in Madīnah, such that they did not realize that he was the one feeding them until he passed away.[336]

It has been reported that a Zoroastrian (*majūsī*) came to Ibrāhīm ؑ seeking hospitality. Ibrāhīm allegedly told him, 'I will host you upon the condition that you become Muslim.' The Zoroastrian refused, then turned away. Then Allah ﷻ reported told Ibrāhīm:

> O Ibrāhīm! Will you not host the Zoroastrian? We have fed him for the past 70 years even though he has been upon disbelief, so how is it a burden upon you, when I host you [as well]?

Thereafter, Ibrāhīm went after the Zoroastrian to inform him that he would host him. The man then asked him, 'What is the reason for your refusal to host me in the first instance, only for you to invite me the second time?' Ibrāhīm then told him that the Truth ﷻ rebuked him concerning his responsibility towards hosting him. The man replied, 'Really? Is this why you are doing this for me? Give me your hand.' At this, the Zoroastrian became Muslim at the hand of Ibrāhīm.[337]

As the *fatā* should honour his neighbours, he is obliged to also honour guests, including wayfarers. Once again, Allah ﷻ relates an account of Ibrāhīm in *Surah al-Dhāriyāt*, verses 24-28:

> Has the story of the honoured guests of Ibrāhīm reached you?
>
> Remember when they entered his presence and greeted him with 'Peace'. He replied, 'Peace.' Then he said to himself, 'these are an unfamiliar people'.
>
> Then he went to his family and came with a fat [roasted] calf.
>
> And placed it before them, asking, 'Will you not eat?'

So, he grew apprehensive of them. They reassured him, 'Do not be afraid', and gave him good news of a knowledgeable son [Isma'īl].

This narration is also present in *Surah Hūd*, verses 69 and 70:

And certainly, did Our messengers come to Ibrāhīm with good tidings; they said, 'Peace.' He said, 'Peace', and did not delay in bringing [them] a roasted calf.

But when he saw their hands not reaching for it, he distrusted them and felt apprehension from them. They said, 'Fear not. We have been sent to the People of Lūṭ.'

In both instances, Ibrāhīm ﷺ had guests that he did not know were angels; hence, they did not eat, as angels do not consume food. It was clearly the hospitality of Ibrāhīm that caused him to feed his guests the best food available, whether he knew them or not. Allah continues the narrative in the 77th to 79th verses of this surah:

And when Our messengers came to Lūṭ, he was anguished for them and felt for them great discomfort and said, 'This is a trying day.'

And the men of his people hastened to him. He pleaded, 'O my people! Here are my daughters [for marriage]—they are pure for you. So be mindful of Allah, and do not humiliate me by disrespecting my guests. Is there not even a single righteous man among you?'

They argued, 'You certainly know that we have no need for your daughters. You already know what we desire!'

In these circumstances, Lūṭ ﷺ stood up for the honour of his guests, angels who were not to be disrespected or subjected to inappropriate and shameful propositions. This event exemplifies the saying of Imam 'Alī when he stated, 'Hospitality is the head of manly honour.'[338] Indeed, on the topic of hospitality, the Prophet ﷺ stated:

> He who believes in Allah and the Last Day should honour his neighbour. He who believes in Allah and the Last Day should take great care of the *jāi'zah* of his guest.
>
> The narrator asked: What is his *jā'izah*[339], O Messenger of Allah?
>
> The Prophet replied: His *jā'izah* extends over one day and one night while (general) hospitality extends over three days. And beyond that is counted as *ṣadaqah*. And he who believes in Allah and the last day should speak a good word or keep silent.[340]

It was reported that Imam 'Alī was crying one day, so he was asked, 'What makes you cry?' He replied, 'A guest has not come to me in seven days, so I fear that Allah is disgracing me.'[341]

“NONE OF YOU BELIEVES UNTIL HE LOVES FOR HIS BROTHER WHAT HE LOVES FOR HIMSELF FROM GOODNESS.”

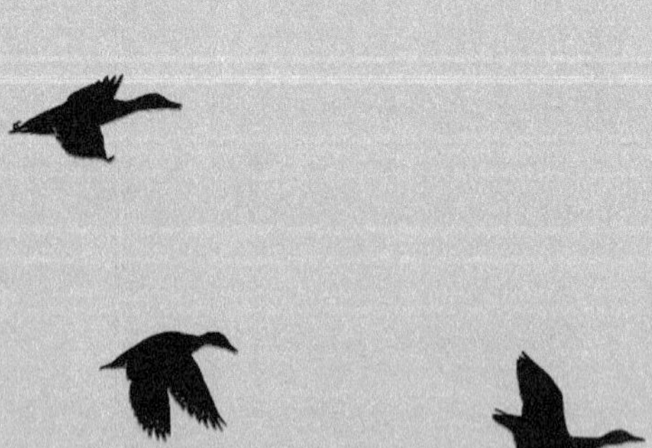

Honourable

Altruism

Of the foremost aspects of *futuwwah* is altruism, which contains the honourable quality of one preferring others over himself. The *fatā*, in his altruism, would rather others have something than himself, being willing to take abuse and insults, yet not wishing to return it to the one who insults him. His manliness is embodied in his generosity that goes beyond sharing what he has; his true worship is that he takes to self-sacrifice and preferring others over himself.[342]

The Prophet ﷺ said, 'None of you believes until he loves for his brother what he loves for himself from goodness.'[343] In reality, this means that the believer does not only want his brother to have what he has, but that he wants his brother to have more than what he has, according to his highest aspirations of obtaining goodness. The Prophet ﷺ possesses the highest level of honorific altruism. Al-Daqqāq said:

> This characteristic is not perfected in anyone except the Messenger of Allah ﷺ. Surely everyone on the Day of Resurrection will say, 'Myself, myself!' But he will say, 'My Ummah, my Ummah!'[344]

Imam ʿAlī ibn Abī Ṭālib ﷺ displayed his altruism in the well-known event when the Prophet ﷺ, along with Abū Bakr ﷺ, escaped from Makkah to migrate to Madinah. When the ignorant elders of Quraysh came together and plotted to kill the Prophet ﷺ, they agreed that a man from each tribe would take part in the assassination of the Prophet ﷺ; thus, a single tribe would not have to take the sole responsibility. Jibrīl ﷺ informed the Prophet ﷺ that they were going to attempt to kill him that night. Imam ʿAlī told him, 'I, O Messenger of Allah, I will give myself; I will stay in your bed tonight.' When night fell, the men came for the Prophet ﷺ but found Imam ʿAlī instead.[345]

Another such example of altruism occurred during the era of the government of ʿUmar ibn al-Khaṭṭāb ﷺ in the famous Battle of al-Yarmūk, in which the Muslims fought against the Byzantines. During the battle, it is narrated that three Companions of the Prophet ﷺ were gravely injured. Al-Ḥārith ibn Hishām asked for water, then looked towards ʿIkrimah ibn Abī Jahl, and said that water should go to him before himself. ʿIkrimah then looked over to ʿAyyāsh ibn Abī Rabīʿah and said to give the water to ʿAyyāsh before himself. When the water was brought to ʿAyyāsh, he passed away, then the man with the water looked over to Al-Ḥārith to give him water, but he passed away as well. Finally, he looked to ʿIkrimah to give him water only for him to pass away as well.[346] Such was the nobility and altruism of the Companions!

Allah ﷻ stated in *Surah al-Ḥashr,* verse 9:

> *And [also for] those who were settled in the Home [Madinah] and accepted the faith before them, they love those who emigrated to them and do not find any want in their breasts of what they were given, but prefer them [emigrants] over themselves, even though they find poverty as their lot. And whoever is protected from the stinginess of his own soul, those are the successful people.*

Though the helpers themselves were in need, they preferred the emigrants over themselves with their property and material wealth. Al-Tustarī ﷺ said, 'They preferred them, for the felicity of Allah over their own desires, and their altruism was a confirmation of their love.'[347] Ibn 'Aṭā' said, 'They preferred generosity over their wealth and themselves, even though they were in need (i.e. hungry).'[348]

Speaking of stinginess, the opposite of altruism, Ibn Mas'ūd ﷺ stated:

> It is not that extreme stinginess relates to one not making ritual remembrance (*dhikr*) of Allah, but rather, extreme stinginess is wrongfully taking the wealth of your brother, and that is stingy. And the worst thing is stinginess.[349]

His statement conveys the meaning that, from a spiritual sense, not giving one's wealth and food to his brother is taking away from him what should be viewed with the heart as rightfully his. Describing the altruistic believers, Allah ﷻ said in *Surah al-Insān*, verses 8-13:

> *And they give food in spite of love for it to the needy, the orphan, and the captive,*
>
> *[Saying], 'We feed you only for the countenance of Allah. We wish not from you reward nor thanks.*
>
> *Surely, we fear from our Lord a Day austere and distressful.'*
>
> *So, Allah will protect them from the evil of that Day and give them radiance and happiness.*
>
> *And will reward them for what they patiently endured [with] a garden [in Paradise] and silk [garments].*
>
> *[They will be] reclining therein on adorned couches. They will not see therein any [burning] sun nor [freezing] cold.*

It has been reported that the occasion of this revelation relates to Imam 'Alī, Fāṭimah, al-Ḥasan, and al-Ḥusayn ﷺ. Reportedly, Imam

ʿAlī and Fāṭimah fasted and made their food for breaking fast, only for a needy person to come to their door and ask for food, so they gave him their food. They fasted the following day, but before the time to break their fast came, an orphan came to the door begging for food, so they gave him their food. They fasted the following day, and once more, before the time to break their fast came, a prisoner of war was released and came to them asking for food, and they gave him their iftar just as they had the previous two days.[350] They preferred those who were not their kin – including a prisoner who was not a Muslim – over themselves, only breaking their fast with water for three consecutive days.

It was also reported that the Prophet ﷺ had a guest come then he said, 'Whoever honours my guest, I guarantee for him that Allah will grant him paradise.' Imam ʿAlī reportedly responded, 'I will, O Messenger of Allah.' So, he took the guest home to Fāṭimah ؑ while there was barely enough food for everyone. When darkness fell, the iftar food was prepared and placed in front of the guest and ʿAlī. Then, Fāṭimah came to the light and extinguished it, after which ʿAlī took her by the hand and left the guest to eat the food while ʿAlī and Fāṭimah did not eat anything – though both fasted that day.[351]

Imam Jaʿfār al-Sādiq ؑ was once asked about *futuwwah*:[352]

> The Imam responded to him, asking, 'What do you say?'
>
> The inquirer responded, 'If when I am given, I am thankful, but if I am denied, I am patient.'
>
> The Imam replied, 'The dogs with us are like this.'
>
> The man then inquired, 'O son of the Messenger of Allah! What is *futuwwah* with you [Ahl al-Bayt]?'
>
> He said, 'If we are given, we give it away in preference to others, but if we are denied, we are still grateful.'

Likewise, Al-Ḥārith al-Muḥāsibī ﷺ said, '*Futuwwah* is that you are just without demanding justice for yourself, and that you give and do not take.'[353] Abū Bakr al-Warrāq stated, 'The *fatā* is he who is not an antagonist.'[354] This means that he is not antagonistic towards others simply because they are adversarial towards him, for it is said that it is from *futuwwah* for one to cover the faults of his adversary, just as they would want their faults covered, regardless of if their faults may have been exposed by their adversaries.[355]

Once a man fell asleep in the masjid in al-Madinah and awoke presuming that his money was stolen. He then saw Imam Jaʿfār al-Sādiq praying close by, so he grabbed him. The following then transpired:

> The Imam asked him, 'What is the matter?'
>
> The man said, 'My money was stolen, and there is no one around here with me beside you!'
>
> The Imam said, 'How much was your money?'
>
> The man replied, 'A thousand gold coins!'
>
> The Imam then told him, 'Come with me to my house, so I can give you a thousand gold coins.'

The man came with him and was given a thousand gold coins by the Imam. When the man came back to his friends and relayed the story, they told him that his money was with them. The man then asked who the Imam was, not knowing his identity, so they told him, 'Surely he is the son of the Messenger of Allah.' The man went to the Imam, kissed his feet, and asked for his pardon, attempting to return the thousand gold coins, but the Imam would not accept the money back, saying 'What we give is for the sake of Allah, so it cannot be returned to us.'[356]

Finally, al-Junayd ﷺ said, '*futuwwah* is in ceasing [to reply] to insults and spending [for others] magnanimously.'[357]

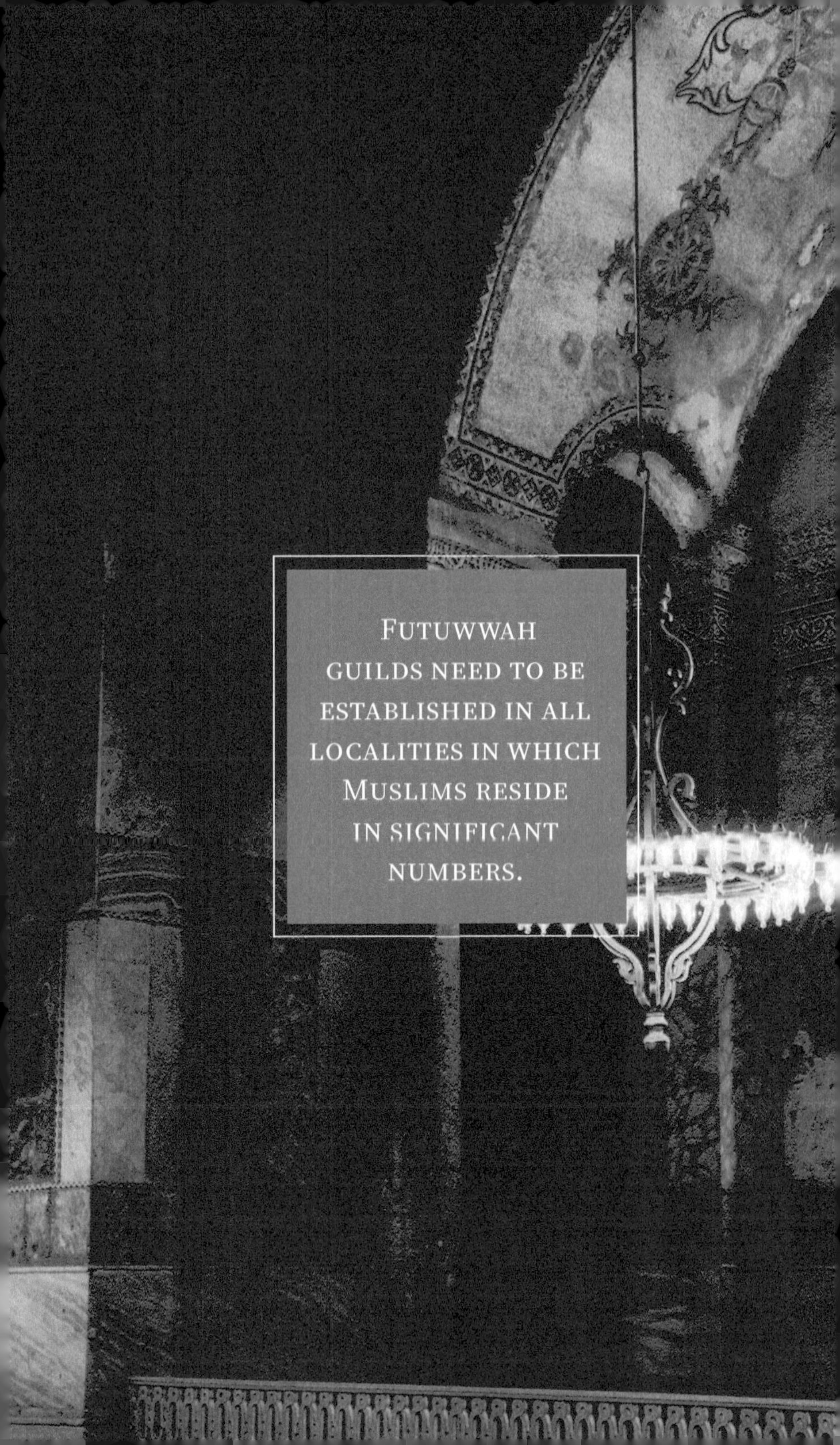

FUTUWWAH GUILDS NEED TO BE ESTABLISHED IN ALL LOCALITIES IN WHICH MUSLIMS RESIDE IN SIGNIFICANT NUMBERS.

Conclusion

This book was intended to be a supplemental text related to the raising of young males to be chivalrous men according to select Islamic spiritual precepts. It was not meant to take the place of qualified teachers and guides who have sat with their predecessors who are connected to chains of transmission from which they learned noble, manly comportment, and the spiritual science of the purification of the heart.

I did not elucidate on matters of theology or creed in this book, although such matters are extremely important. Moreover, I only touched on a few aspects that related to Islamic sacred law. This was intentional, not by omission. Part of the crises of manhood in the West in general - not just with Muslims - stems from the erosion of manners and the diminishment of noble traits of character that are the foundation of ethics. Hence, I was more concerned with highlighting examples of beautiful comportment in speech and actions for the sake of Allah ﷻ, which some may categorize as virtue ethics.

Beautiful comportment, however, cannot be learned exclusively from any book. It is something that is learned from the lived experiences of men whose spiritual states exude an embodiment of noble manliness. Part of the challenge of Muslims in the West face is to invest in structures through which young males can learn some comportment through repeated interaction with living and breathing souls. This is true for youth who have fathers in their lives, but is even more necessary for the countless and growing number of young males who do not have the presence of fathers in their lives.

Our priorities need to be reordered in regard to how we teach Islam to youth. Learning proper comportment must take priority before attempting to teach theology or the specifics of jurisprudential rulings. Imam Mālik ibn Anas famously said to a *fatā* from Quraysh, 'O nephew! Learn comportment before you attempt to learn sacred knowledge.'[358] And it was said:

> The intellectual without comportment is like a brave warrior without a weapon. The intellect and comportment are like the spirit. A body without a spirit is a lifeless form, and a spirit without a body is wind.

Imam Zayd ibn ʿAlī ibn al-Ḥusayn ibn ʿAlī ibn Abī Ṭālib also stated, 'O man! Be a brother of comportment whether you are from the non-Arabs or Arabs. Surely the *fatā* is he who says he has comportment; the *fatā* is not he who says that he refuses it.'

Again, my comments about the importance of comportment are not to downplay the necessity of learning sound theology and basic jurisprudential obligations. It is to say, however, that there can be no renewal of sacred manhood without this emphasis.

Likewise, the importance of an orderly teaching of spiritual purification must be revived. In America in particular, there have been decades of dry inculcation of Islamic teachings as polemical theology, rigid interpretations of what constitutes heresy, blameworthy religious innovation, and telling stories about select historical Muslim personalities void of contemporary correlation, which are at times even discussed in ahistorical, exaggerated terms. The lack of a spiritual connection in many Muslims who were raised in this limbo has led to faux spiritual connectivity through philosophies based outside of Islam, or based solely in individualistic feelings.

Of course, the revival of sacred manhood has a metaphysical component which must be connected to theology. Allah ﷻ said in *Surah Āl ʿImrān,* verse 36: *'And the male is not like the female.'* The Prophet ﷺ said, 'To everything is a deeper reality.'[359] The differences between males and females goes beyond outward physiological distinctions, also including metaphysical realities. Unfortunately, many Muslims have been influenced by what secular materialists have proposed, explanations that attempt to reduce our understanding of humans to be evolved mammals that react to stimuli. The realities of both manhood and womanhood are based upon the natural inclinations of primordial selves towards traits of spiritual majesty and spiritual beauty. The incumbency for instruction in this topic, not just for youth but even for many adults above the age of forty that are thoroughly confused, must also be robustly and courageously taught.

It is my belief that *futuwwah* guilds need to be established in all localities in which Muslims reside in significant numbers. The Boy Scouts of America, though it has some beneficial aspects, should not be our go-to organization for renewing sacred manhood. For one, the Boy Scouts is not centred around organized religious beliefs which are incontrovertible. That the Boy Scouts now allow 'gender neutral' scouts in and of itself introduces a serious problem into gatherings that purport to instil ethics and cultivate brotherhood. Another point is that manners taught by the Boys Scouts are deficient in comparison to the comportment that we should strive to embody and teach, which is the way of our Prophet ﷺ that has been transmitted and survives today among the saints and the righteous. Muslims have the responsibility of forming our own guilds and lodges based upon our own tradition instead of seeking to be led by others. This, in and of itself, is part of reviving sacred manhood.

Futuwwah guilds can look slightly different based upon their locations and demographics, but should have some common components, such as:

1) Structured circles with upright teachers through which young males can learn comportment and spiritual purification.

2) Different rankings within guilds, such that there are rites of passage before members can move on to next phases. Young males who graduate to their next levels should be paired off to be peer mentors for those who are younger. I saw this while in Dogon Country, Mali, in which young males were taken to a special area and taught manliness, after which they came back to their villages recognized as young men with greater responsibilities within society.

3) Group physical activities to instil discipline and establish a sense of brotherhood. This should include teaching martial arts and archery within guilds. When possible, this should also include the aspect of learning how to hunt and skin animals (such as deer) according to Islamic law.

4) Organized activities of weekly community service such as helping the elderly, delivering food boxes to the poor, shovelling snow for widows, etc.

Besides these aspects, some localities may wish to organize artisan skills or crafts that can be taught, so that young men can have a way to make some income for themselves that they are not exclusively dependent on others giving them jobs. This was an aspect of the *futuwwah* guilds during the era of the Abbasid Khalīfah al-Nāṣir li Dīn Allah ﷺ.

Approximately three years ago, a group of brothers in Detroit, Michigan known as the Ansar Collective began *futuwwah* sessions, teaching the *Kitāb al-Futuwwah* of al-Sulamī, which expanded into opportunities for regular community service along with bi-weekly martial arts classes. The Ansar Collective, which is composed of Imam Saleem Khalid, who is our elder and leader, Sheikh Abdul Karim Yahya, Sheikh Kafani Cisse, Imam Seifullah Shakoor, Ustadh Shakir Bakari-Williams, Brother Jermaine Carey, Brother Khalil

Mu'minun, Brother Jabril Aḥmad, and I, started these sessions at Dar al-Rahma Zāwiyah in Detroit. The gatherings, which are multi-ethnic and inter-generational, have served as a platform for younger brothers to discuss sensitive topics in male-only spaces in which we operate from the principle of 'what is said in gatherings stays in those gatherings'. Through the relationship of Sheikh Abdul Karim Yahya with Sheikh Ibrahim Osi-Efa who also studied in Tarim, Yemen, we have also been kept abreast of the noble efforts of our brothers in the Futuwwa Initiative in Peterborough, England. We also know of a few other groups, including The Karima Foundation (also in England), that are involved in this noble endeavour.

It is my hope that, in addition to this book being a simple resource, it may add to the spark for a movement to re-establish *futuwwah* among our young men that was lit a few years ago with the *Resurrection: Ertugrul* Turkish television series, which clearly showed aspects of Islamic chivalry and sacred manhood without explicitly using the term *futuwwah*. Perhaps we may even one day establish an international network of guilds and lodges based upon restoring sacred manhood through the grace of Allah ﷻ.

May Allah forgive me, forgive you, and forgive all Muslims, for surely He is Oft-Forgiving, the Merciful Redeemer.

Notes

1 Al-Tirmidhī, *Al-Shamā'il al-Muḥammadiyyah,* Hadith 374.

2 Moore and Gillette, *King Warrior Magician Lover: Rediscovering the Archetypes of the Mature Masculine,* New edition, p. 4.

3 Abd-Allah, 'Islam and the Cultural Imperative', p. 14.

4 Muslim, *Ṣaḥīḥ Muslim,* Hadith 2664.

5 Al-Nawawī, *Al-Minhāj fī Sharḥ Ṣaḥīḥ Muslim ibn al-Ḥajjāj.*

6 Ridgeon, *Jawanmardi: A Sufi Code of Honour*, pp. 1–14.

7 Amīn, *Al-Sal'akah wa al-Futuwwah fī al-Islām.*

8 S. Z. Chowdhury, *A Sufi Apologist of Nishapur: The Life and Thought of Abū 'Abd al-Raḥmān Al-Sulamī* (Sheffield, UK; Bristol, CT: Equinox Publishing Ltd, 2019).

9 Ibn Qayyim al-Jawziyyah, *Madārij al-Sālikīn*, vol. 2 (Cairo: Dār al-Hadith, 2005), p. 278.

10 Amin, *Al-Sal'akah wa al-Futuwwah fī al-Islām, pp.* 30–38.

11 Ibn Battuta, *The Travels of Ibn Battuta: In the Near East, Asia and Africa, 1325-1354,* p. 102.

12 Azzam, *Saladin: The Triumph of the Sunni Revival,* 2nd New edition, p. 48.

13 Al-Khaṭīb, *Al-Buṭūlah wa al-Fidā 'Inda al-Ṣūfiyyah,* 5th ed, pp. 65, 178.

14 Vaid, *On Muslim Masculinity,* Medium, 22 January 2021 https://medium.com/occasionalreflections/on-muslim-masculinity-1c39bf8eaa0f; Zimbardo, *Man Disconnected: How the Digital Age Is Changing Young Men Forever*

15 Zimbardo, *Man Disconnected,* pp. 87–137.

16 Harrington, *The Desperation behind OnlyFans,* UnHerd, 3 December 2020, https://unherd.com/2020/12/the-desperation-behind-onlyfans/.

17 Zimbardo, *Man Disconnected.*

18 Aḥmad, *Graduating towards Marriage? Attitudes towards Marriage and Relationships among University-Educated British Muslim Women, Culture and Religion* 13, no. 2 (1 June 2012): 193–210, https://doi.org/10.1080/14755610.2012.674953; Islam UK, *Dr Fauzia Aḥmad: 'The British Muslim Marriage Crisis'*, 2019, https://www.youtube.com/watch?v=mGnsvEndD3U.

19 'Asian Grooming: Why We Need to Talk about Sex', The Independent, 11 May 2012, https://www.independent.co.uk/news/uk/crime/asian-grooming-why-we-need-talk-about-sex-7734712.html.

20 Brown, *An Open Letter to Muslim Men: The Sunnah Trumps Toxic Masculinity,* Yaqeen Institute for Islamic Research, accessed 2 February 2021, https://yaqeeninstitute.org/jonathan-brown/an-open-letter-to-muslim-men-the-sunnah-trumps-toxic-masculinity.

21 Abdal Hakim Murad, *Travelling Home: Essays on Islam in Europe,* p. 8.

22 Ibn al-Qayyim, *al-Jawāb al-Kāfi,* p. 144.

23 Murad, *Commentary on the Eleventh Contentions,* p. 37.

24 Nadwi, *Prophet of Mercy: Nabiyy-i Rahmat.*

25 Quilliam, 'The Importance of Being Rugged', *Traversing Tradition* (blog), 28 September 2020, https://traversingtradition.com/2020/09/28/the-importance-of-being-rugged/.

26 Al-Ghazālī, *Iḥyā' 'Ulūm al-Dīn,* vol. 2, p. 299.

27 Al-Ḥākim, *Al-Mustadrak 'alā al-Ṣaḥīḥayn,* Hadith 8699.

28 Sukayrij, *Kashf al-Ḥijāb*, p. 105

29 Al-Jīlānī, *Kitāb al-Bulbul al-Ṣādī bi Mawlid al-Hādī*, p. 26

30 Al-Nawawī, *Al-Minhāj fi Sharḥ Ṣaḥīḥ Muslim ibn al-Ḥajjāj,* Hadith 867

31 Al-Suyūṭī, *Sunan al-Nasa'ī bi Sharḥ al-Suyūṭī wa Hāshiyah al-Sanad,* Hadith 1578.

32 Khachaturian, *Ahl al-Futuwwah wa al-Fityān fī al-Mujtamā' al-Islāmī*, pp. 17-25.

33 Al-Nawawī, *Al-Minhāj fī Sharḥ Ṣaḥīḥ Muslim ibn al-Ḥajjāj,* Hadith 2204.

34 Ibn Mufliḥ, *Al-Ādāb al-Shar'iyyah wa al-Minaḥ al-Mar'iyyah,* vol. 2, p. 232.

35 Ibn Manẓūr, *Lisān al-'Arab,* vol. 3, p. 2986.

36 Al-Kasnazān, *Mawsū'ah al-Kasnazān fīmā Aṣṭalaḥa 'Alayhi Ahl al-Taṣawwuf wa al-'Irfān,* vol. 17, p. 210.

37 Al-Jurjānī, *Al-I'tibār wa Salwah al-'Ārifīn,* p. 168.

38 Ibn Manẓūr, *Lisān al-'Arab,* v, 3, p. 2986.

39 Al-Bukhārī, *Al-Adab al-Mufrad,* Hadith 209.

40 Al-Zamakhsharī, *Asās al-Balāghah,* vol. 2, p. 7.

41 Al-Ardabīlī, *al-Futuwwah,* pp. 4-5.

42 Ibn al-Mi'mār, *Kitāb al-Futuwwah,* p. 139.

43 Ibn al-Miʿmār, *Kitāb al-Futuwwah,* pp. 123-124.

44 Al-Kasnazān, *Mawsūʿah al-Kasnazān fīmā Aṣṭalaha ʿAlayhi Ahl al-Taṣawwuf wa al-ʿIrfān,* vol. 17, p. 213.

45 Ibn al-Miʿmār, *Kitāb al-Futuwwah,* p. 143.

46 Al-Kasnazān, *Mawsūʿah al-Kasnazān fīmā Aṣṭalaḥa ʿAlayhi Ahl al-Taṣawwuf wa al-ʿIrfān,* vol. 17, p. 213.

47 Ibid, p. 225.

48 Ibid, p. 217.

49 Al-Qāshānī, *Adab al-Ṭarīqah wa Asrār al-Ḥaqīqah,* p. 13.

50 Zayd ibn ʿAlī, *Tafsīr Gharīb al-Qur'ān,* p. 426.

51 Al-Ardabīlī, *Futuwwah,* p. 7.

52 Al-Ghumārī, *ʿAlī ibn Abī Ṭālib Imām al-ʿĀrifīn,* p. 86.

53 Ibn Abī al-Ḥadīd, *Sharḥ Nahj al-Balāghah,* vol. 1, p. 5.

54 Ibn al-Ṣabbāgh, *Al-Fuṣūl al-Muhimmah,* p. 31.

55 Al-Nasa'ī, *Kitāb Khaṣā'iṣ Amīr al-Mu'minīn ʿAlī ibn Abī Ṭālib,* Hadith 2.

56 Ibn al-Jawzī, *Manāqib al-Imām Aḥmad,* p.163.

57 Al-Ḥaskanī, *Shawāhid al-Tanzīl,* p. 123.

58 Al-Ḥākim, *Faḍā'il Fāṭimah al-Zahrā',* p. 24.

59 Ibid.

60 Al-Jazarī, *Asmā al-Manāqib fī Tahdhib Asnā al-Maṭālib fī Manāqib al-Imām Amīr al-Mu'minīn ʿAlī ibn Abī Ṭālib,* pp. 32-33.

61 Al-Ardabīlī, *Futuwwah,* p. 6; Al-Miʿmār, *Kitāb al-Futuwwah,* p. 126.

62 Ridgeon, *Jawanmardi: A Sufi Code of Honour,* p. 45.

63 Al-Miʿmār, *Kitāb al-Futuwwah,* p. 127.

64 Ibid, p. 124.

65 Al-Thāmirī and al-Qadḥāt, *Rasā'il min al-Turāth al-Ṣūfī fī Labs al-Khirqah,* pp. 223-224.

66 Al-Nāqib, *Siyāsah al-Khalīfah al-Nāṣir li Dīn Allah al-Dākhīliyyah,* pp. 101-111.

67 Al-Fayyūmī, *Al-Miṣbāḥ al-Munīr fī Gharīb al-Sharḥ al-Kabīr,* p. 376.

68 Al-Kasnazān, *Mawsūʿah al-Kasnazān fīmā Aṣṭalaḥa ʿAlayhi Ahl al-Taṣawwuf wa al-ʿIrfān,* vol. 13, p. 144.

69 Ibid.

70 Al-Jīlānī, *Kitāb al-Futuwwah fī Kafiyyah Akh al-ʿAhd wa al-Bayʿah,* pp. 212-213.

71 Al-Bukhārī, *Saḥīḥ al-Bukhārī,* Hadith #6094; Muslim, *Ṣaḥīḥ Muslim,* hadith 2607.

72 Al-Tamīmī, *Ghurār al-Ḥikam wa Durar al-Kalim,* p. 174.

73 Ibid.

74 Al-Qāshānī, *Adab al-Ṭarīqah wa Asrār al-Ḥaqīqah,* p. 29.

75 Ibid.

76 Al-Anṣārī, *Manāzil al-Sā'irīn,* p. 248.

77 Al-Bukhārī, *Saḥīḥ al-Bukhārī,* Hadith 1; *Ṣaḥīḥ Muslim,* Hadith 1907.

78 Al- Dhammarī, *Kitāb Taṣfīyah al-Qulūb,* p. 338.

79 Al-Tamīmī, *Ghurār al-Ḥikam wa Durar al-Kalim* p. 360.

80 Al-Kasnazān, *Mawsū'ah al-Kasnazān fīmā Aṣṭalaḥa 'Alayhi Ahl al-Taṣawwuf wa al-'Irfān,* vol. 20, p. 449.

81 Ibid, vol. 7, p. 217.

82 Ibid, vol. 20, p. 448.

83 Ibid p. 443.

84 Al-Darqāwī, *Rasā'il Mawlay al-'Arab al-Darqāwī,* p. 53.

85 Al-Qāshānī, *Adab al-Ṭarīqah wa Asrār al-Ḥaqīqah,* p. 29

86 Al-Dhammarī, *Taṣfīyah al-Qulūb,* pp. 340-341.

87 Al-Tamīmī, *Ghurār al-Ḥikam wa Durar al-Kalim,* p. 174.

88 Ibid, p. 175.

89 'Izzān, *Majmū' Kutub wa Rasā'il al-Imām Zayd ibn 'Alī,* p. 168.

90 Al-Kasnazān, *Mawsū'ah al-Kasnazān fīmā Aṣṭalaḥa 'Alayhi Ahl al-Taṣawwuf wa al-'Irfān,* vol. 13, p. 152.

91 Al-Zu'bī, *Itḥāf al-Akābir fī Sīrah wa Manāqib al-Imām Muḥyī al-Dīn 'Abd al-Qādir al-Jīlanī al-Ḥasanī al-Ḥusaynī* , p.160.

92 Al-Qāshānī, *Adab al-Ṭarīqah wa Asrār al-Ḥaqīqah,* p. 29

93 Ibid, p. 30.

94 Ibn Kathīr, *Al-Fuṣūl fī Sīrah al-Rasūl,* p. 82.

95 Al-Būṭī, *Fiqh al-Sunnah al-Nabawiyyah,* p. 106.

96 Al-Dhammarī, *Taṣfīyah al-Qulūb,* p.340.

97 Al-Jīlānī, *Al-Ghunyah,* p. 502.

98 Al-Kasnazān, *Mawsū'ah al-Kasnazān fīmā Aṣṭalaḥa 'Alayhi Ahl al-Taṣawwuf wa al-'Irfān,* vol. 13, p. 167.

99 Al-Kasnazān, *Mawsū'ah al-Kasnazān fīmā Aṣṭalaḥa 'Alayhi Ahl al-Taṣawwuf wa al-'Irfān,* vol. 6, p. 17.

100 Ibid, p. 23.

101 Ibid. p. 88.

102 Al-Kubaysī, *Mawsū'ah al-Kalimah wa Akhawātihā fī al-Qur'ān al-Karīm,* vol. 3, p. 5.

103 Al-Sayyadī, *Bawāriq al-Ḥaqā'iq,* p. 47.

104 Abū Dāwūd, *Sunan Abī Dāwūd,* Hadith 4681.

105 Al-Sayyadī, *Bawāriq al-Ḥaqā'iq,* p. 34.

106 Al-Sha'rānī, *Al-Ṭabaqāt al-Kubrā*, p. 32.

107 Al-Jīlānī, *Al-Fatḥ al-Rabbānī wa al-Fayḍ al-Rahmānī*, p. 108.

108 Al-Kasnazān, *Mawsū'ah al-Kasnazān fīmā Aṣṭalaḥa 'Alayhi Ahl al-Taṣawwuf wa al-'Irfān*, vol. 15, p. 14.

109 Al-Sha'rānī, *Al-Ṭabaqāt al-Kubrā*, p. 32.

110 Al-Sakhāwī, *Ṭabaqāt al-Awliyā' al-Mukarramīn*, vol. 1, p. 69.

111 Ibid, p. 262.

112 Al-Wāsiṭī, *Al-Burhān al-Mu'ayyid li Ṣāḥib Madd al-Yad Mawlāna al-Ghawth al-Sharīf al-Rifā'ī Aḥmad*, p. 117.

113 Ibn Mājah, *Sunan Ibn Mājah*, Hadith 4102.

114 Ibn Aḥmad, *Al-Ṭarā'if al-Mushtaqīn min Qaṣaṣ al-Awliyā' wa al-Ṣāliḥīn*, p. 112.

115 Al-'Āmilī, *Al-Kashkūl*, vol. 1, p. 15.

116 Al-Sakhāwī, *Ṭabaqāt al-Awliyā' al-Mukarramīn*, vol. 1, p. 68.

117 Al-'Āmilī, *Al-Kashkūl*, vol. 1, p. 256.

118 Al-Tirmidhī, *Sunan al-Tirmidhī*, Hadith 3616.

119 Ibn Ḥanbal, *Musnad Aḥmad*, Hadith 18067.

120 Muslim, *Ṣaḥīḥ Muslim*, Hadith 7331.

121 Ibn Mūsā, *Al-Shifā' bi Ta'rīf Huqūq al-Muṣṭafā*, p.15.

122 Al-Qushayrī, *Al-Risālah al-Qushayriyyah fī 'Ilm al-Taṣawwuf*, p.217

123 Al-Haythamī, *Majma' al-Zawā'id*, v.10, p.123.

124 Al-Jīlānī, *Al-Fatḥ al-Rabbānī wa al-Fayḍ al-Raḥmānī*, p. 117.

125 Al-Jīlānī, *Tafsīr al-Jīlānī*, v.4, pp. 377-378.

126 Al-Ṭabarānī, *Al-Mu'jam al-Kabīr*, Hadith 2641.

127 Al-Ṭabarānī, *Al-Mu'jam al-Awsāṭ*, Hadith 2155; al-Hākim, *Al-Mustadrak 'ala al-Ṣaḥiḥayn*, Hadith 4802.

128 Al-Ṭabarī, *Tafsīr Al-Ṭabarī*, vol. 11, p. 144.

129 Al-Sha'rānī, *Al-Ṭabaqāt al-Kubrā*, p.48.

130 Al-Jīlānī, *Kitāb al-Bulbul al-Ṣādī bi Mawlid al-Hādī*, p.30.

131 Niasse, *Fī Riyāḍ al-Tafsīr li al-Qur'ān al-Karīm*, vol. 5, p. 382.

132 Al-Suyūṭī, *Al-Jāmi' al-Saghīr*, Hadith 1686.

133 Ibid, Hadith 4680.

134 Al-Iskandarī, *Al-'Amāl al-Kāmilah*, p. 265.

135 Ibn Ḥanbal, *Musnad Aḥmad*, Hadith 25234.

136 Al-Tirmidhī, *Sunan al-Tirmidhī*, Hadith 3490.

137 Al-Kasnazān, *Mawsū'ah al-Kasnazān fīmā Aṣṭalaḥa 'Alayhi Ahl al-Taṣawwuf wa al-'Irfān*, vol. 17, p. 154.

138 Al-Bukhārī, *Saḥīḥ al-Bukhārī*, Hadith 5223; Muslim, *Ṣaḥīḥ Muslim*, Hadith 2761; Al-Tirmidhī, *Sunan al-Tirmidhī*, Hadith 1168.

139 Al-Bukhārī, *Saḥīḥ Al-Bukhārī,* Hadith 4634; Muslim, *Ṣaḥīḥ Muslim,* Hadith 2760; Al-Tirmidhī, *Sunan al-Tirmidhī,* Hadith 3530.

140 Al-Tamīmī, *Ghurār al-Ḥikam wa Durar al-Kalim,* p. 209.

141 Ibid.

142 Ibn Abī Shaybah, *Al-Muṣannaf,* Hadith 38573.

143 Ibn Manẓūr, *Lisān al-ʿArab,* p. 2958.

144 Al-Ṣanʿānī, *Tafsīr ʿAbd al-Razzāq,* vol. 3, p. 324.

145 ʿIṭr, *Al-Kāfī fī Fiqh al-Shāfiʿī,* p. 60.

146 Al-Sayyadī, *Bawāriq al-Ḥaqā'iq,* p. 40.

147 Ibn Manẓūr, *Lisān al-ʿArab,* p. 2958.

148 Ibn al-Miʿmār, *Kitāb al-Futuwwah,* p. 159.

149 Al-Nasa'ī, *Sunan al-Nasa'ī,* Hadith 2562; Ibn Ḥanbal, *Musnad Aḥmad,* Hadith 6180.

150 Al-Kasnazān, *Mawsūʿah al-Kasnazān fīmā Aṣṭalaḥa ʿAlayhi Ahl al-Taṣawwuf wa al-ʿIrfān,* vol. 22, p. 79.

151 Ibid.

152 Al-Ardabīlī, *Futuwwah,* p. 11.

153 Ibid, p. 14.

154 Al-Tirmidhī, *Al-Shamā'il al-Muḥammadiyyah wa al-Khaṣā'il al-Muṣṭafawiyyah,* Hadith 329.

155 Ibn Mājah, *Sunan Ibn Mājah,* Hadith 4308.

156 Ibn Ḥanbal, *Musnad Aḥmad,* Hadith 65790.

157 Al-Bukhārī, *Saḥīḥ Al-Bukhārī,* Hadith 3671.

158 Al-Tirmidhī, *Al-Shamā'il al-Muḥammadiyyah wa al-Khaṣā'il al-Muṣṭafawiyyah,* Hadith 332.

159 Al-Ṭabarī, *Tafsīr Al-Ṭabarī,* vol. 8, p. 210.

160 Ibn Ḥibbān, *Saḥīḥ Ibn Ḥibbān,* Hadith 361.

161 Al-Tirmidhī, *Sunan al-Tirmidhī,* Hadith 3766.

162 Al-Jurjānī, *Al-Iʿtibār wa Salwah al-ʿĀrifīn,* p. 188.

163 Ibid, p. 189.

164 Al-Kasnazān, *Mawsūʿah al-Kasnazān fīmā Aṣṭalaḥa ʿAlayhi Ahl al-Taṣawwuf wa al-ʿIrfān,* vol. 22, p. 80.

165 Ibid, p. 81.

166 Ibid, p. 82.

167 Ibid, p. 92.

168 Al-Kasnazān, *Mawsūʿah al-Kasnazān fīmā Aṣṭalaḥa ʿAlayhi Ahl al-Taṣawwuf wa al-ʿIrfān,* vol. 7, p. 46.

169 Ibid.

170 Al-Daylamī, *Musnad al-Firdaws,* Hadith 3473.

171 Ibn Qayyim, *Zād al-Ma'ād,* p. 38.

172 Ibid.

173 Ibid.

174 Ibid.

175 Ibid.

176 Al-Bukhārī, *Saḥīḥ Al-Bukhārī,* Hadith 143.

177 Fall, *Al-Khidmah 'Inda al-Shaykh al-Khādim Bayna al-Naẓariyyah wa al-Taṭbīq,* p. 61.

178 Al-Kasnazān, *Mawsū'ah al-Kasnazān fīmā Aṣṭalaḥa 'Alayhi Ahl al-Taṣawwuf wa al-'Irfān,* vol. 7, p. 50.

179 Ibid, p. 49.

180 'Izzān, *Majmū' Kutub wa Rasā'il al-Imām Zayd ibn 'Alī,* p. 171.

181 Al-Bukhārī, *Al-Adab al-Mufrad,* p. 17.

182 Al-Jīlānī, *Tafsīr al-Jīlānī,* vol. 4, p. 38.

183 Al-Dhammarī, *Kitāb Taṣfiyah al-Qulūb,* p. 397.

184 Al-Tamīmī, *Ghurār al-Ḥikam wa Durar al-Kalim,* p. 102.

185 Al-Sulamī, *Tafsīr al-Sulamī,* vol. 1, p. 386.

186 Al-Quḍā'ī, *Musnad al-Shihāb,* Hadith 119.

187 Al-Bukhārī, *Al-Adab al-Mufrad,* Hadith 3.

188 Ibid, Hadith 11.

189 Bā Sallūm and Miskā, *Mawsū'ah Āl Bayt al-Nabī,* vol. 2, pp. 422-423.

190 Al-Bukhārī, *Al-Adab al-Mufrad,* Hadith 23.

191 Bā Sallūm and Miskā, *Mawsū'ah Āl Bayt al-Nabī,* vol. 2, p. 423.

192 Al-Bukhārī, *Al-Adab al-Mufrad,* Hadith 60.

193 Al-Tirmidhī, *Sunan al-Tirmidhī,* Hadith 2682; Abū Dāwūd, *Sunan Abī Dāwūd,* Hadith 3641.

194 Rabī'ah, *Rasā'il al-Asmār 'Abd al-Salām ibn Sālim al-Idrīsī Ḥasanī Marīdīh,* pp. 84-85.

195 Al-Tirmidhī, *Sunan al-Tirmidhī,* Hadith 1919.

196 Al-Jīlānī, *Futuwwah,* p. 255.

197 Ibid.

198 Abū Dāwūd, *Sunan Abī Dāwūd,* Hadith 5215.

199 Al-Jīlānī, *Futuwwah,* p. 259.

200 Al-Ṭabarānī, *Al-Mu'jam al-Awsāṭ,* Hadith 6559.

201 Al-Bukhārī, *Al-Mufrad al-Adab,* Hadith 974.

202 Al-Aṣbahānī, *Muḥāḍarāt al-Udabā' wa Muḥāwarāt al-Shu'arā' wa al-Bulaghā',* vol. 1, p. 370.

203 Al-Suhrawardī, *'Awārif al-Ma'ārif*, p. 72.

204 Al-Jīlānī, *Al-Fatḥ al-Rabbānī wa al-Fayḍ al-Rahmānī*, p. 72.

205 Al-Jīlānī, *Kitāb al-Futuwwah fī Kayfiyyah Akhdh al-'Ahd wa al-Bay'ah*, p. 128.

206 Al-Kasnazān, *Mawsū'ah al-Kasnazān fīmā Aṣṭalaḥa 'Alayhi Ahl al-Taṣawwuf wa al-'Irfān*, vol. 11, p. 82.

207 Al-Jīlānī, *Kitāb al-Futuwwah fī Kayfiyyah Akhdh al-'Ahd wa al-Bay'ah*, p. 129.

208 Al-Qāshānī, *Ādāb al-Ṭarīqah wa Asrār al-Ḥaqīqah*, p. 23.

209 Al-Ṭabarānī, *Maqtal al-Ḥusayn ibn 'Alī ibn Abī Ṭālib*, p. 84.

210 Al-Tirmidhī, *Sunan al-Tirmidhī*, Hadith 1961.

211 Al-Ardabīlī, *Futuwwah*, p. 19.

212 Al-Sulamī, *Futuwwah*, p. 9.

213 Ibn Ḥibbān, *Saḥīḥ Ibn Ḥibbān*, Hadith 942.

214 Muslim, *Ṣaḥīḥ Muslim*, Hadith 5726.

215 Al-Kasnazān, *Mawsū'ah al-Kasnazān fīmā Aṣṭalaḥa 'Alayhi Ahl al-Taṣawwuf wa al-'Irfān*, vol. 11, p. 82.

216 Al-Qāshānī, *Ādāb al-Ṭarīqah wa Asrār al-Ḥaqīqah*, p. 22.

217 Al-Jīlānī, *Tafsīr al-Jīlānī*, vol. 1, p. 450.

218 Al-Kasnazān, *Mawsū'ah al-Kasnazān fīmā Aṣṭalaḥa 'Alayhi Ahl al-Taṣawwuf wa al-'Irfān*, vol. 11, p. 82.

219 Al-Dhammarī, *Kitāb Taṣfiyah al-Qulūb*, p. 250.

220 Al-Kasnazān, Mawsū'ah al-Kasnazān fīmā Aṣṭalaḥa 'Alayhi Ahl al-Taṣawwuf wa al-'Irfān, vol. 11, p. 88.

221 Ibid. vol. 4, p. 473.

222 Al-Dhammarī, *Kitāb Taṣfiyah al-Qulūb*, p. 247.

223 Al-Tamīmī, *Ghurār al-Ḥikam wa Durar al-Kalim*, p. 123.

224 Al-Sha'rānī, *Al-Ṭabaqāt al-Kubrā*, p. 41.

225 Al-Aṣbahānī, *Taḥdhīb Ḥilyah al-Awliyā' wa Ṭabaqāt al-Aṣfiyā'*, vol. 1, p. 485.

226 Ibid. p. 490.

227 Al-Jīlānī, *Kitāb al-Futuwwah*, pp. 129-130.

228 Al-Kasnazān, *Mawsū'ah al-Kasnazān fīmā Aṣṭalaḥa 'Alayhi Ahl al-Taṣawwuf wa al-'Irfān*, vol. 5, p. 418.

229 Al-Bukhārī, *Saḥīḥ Al-Bukhārī*, Hadith 6118; Muslim, *Ṣaḥīḥ Muslim*, Hadith 36.

230 Al-Kasnazān, *Mawsū'ah al-Kasnazān fīmā Aṣṭalaḥa 'Alayhi Ahl al-Taṣawwuf wa al-'Irfān*, vol. 5, p. 419.

231 Ibid, p. 428

232 Ibid.

233 Al-Tamīmī, *Ghurār al-Ḥikam wa Durar al-Kalim*, p. 133.

234 Ibid.

235 Al-Bukhārī, *Saḥīḥ Al-Bukhārī,* Hadith #6119.

236 Ibid, Hadith 6120.

237 Al-Kasnazān, *Mawsū'ah al-Kasnazān fīmā Aṣṭalaḥa 'Alayhi Ahl al-Taṣawwuf wa al-'Irfān,* vol. 5, p. 428.

238 Al-Tamīmī, *Ghurār al-Ḥikam wa Durar al-Kalim,* p. 133.

239 Ibid, p. 132.

240 Ibn al-Jawzī, Dhamm al-Hawā, p. 64

241 Al-Kubaysī, *Mawsū'ah al-Kalimah wa Akhawātihā fī al-Qur'ān al-Karīm* vol. 6, p. 691.

242 Dem, *Tafsīr Ḍiyā' al-Nayyirīn al-Jāmi' bayna 'Ulūm al-Tā'ifatayn,* vol. 3, p. 28.

243 Dem, *Tafsīr Ḍiyā' al-Nayyirīn al-Jāmi' bayna 'Ulūm al-Tā'ifatayn,* vol. 3, p. 28.

244 Al-Tirmidhī, *Sunan al-Tirmidhī,* Hadith 2616; Al-Nasa'ī, *Sunan Al-Nasa'ī,* Hadith 11394; Ibn Mājah, *Sunan Ibn Mājah,* Hadith 3973.

245 Al-Kasnazān, *Mawsū'ah al-Kasnazān fīmā Aṣṭalaḥa 'Alayhi Ahl al-Taṣawwuf wa al-'Irfān,* vol. 13, p. 471.

246 Ibid, p. 468.

247 Al-Bukhārī, *Saḥīḥ al-Bukhārī,* Hadith #5065; Muslim; *Ṣaḥīḥ Muslim,* Hadith #1400.

248 Al-Kasnazān, *Mawsū'ah al-Kasnazān fīmā Aṣṭalaḥa 'Alayhi Ahl al-Taṣawwuf wa al-'Irfān,* vol. 13, p. 474.

249 Ibn Fūdī, *Mukhtārāt min Mu'allafāt li al-Shaykh 'Uthmān ibn Fūdī,* p. 17.

250 Al-Bukhārī, *Saḥīḥ Al-Bukhārī,* Hadith 5394; Muslim, *Ṣaḥīḥ Muslim,* Hadith 3060.

251 Al-Sulamī, *Tafsīr al-Sulamī,* vol. 2, p. 43.

252 Bamba, *Diwān al-'Ulūm al-Dīniyyah* p. 432.

253 Al-Bukhārī, *Saḥīḥ Al-Bukhārī,* Hadith 6228; Muslim, *Ṣaḥīḥ Muslim,* Hadith 1334.

254 Al-Bukhārī, *Saḥīḥ Al-Bukhārī,* Hadith 5223; Muslim, *Ṣaḥīḥ Muslim,* Hadith 1334.

255 Al-Tirmidhī, *Sunan al-Tirmidhī,* Hadith 2165.

256 Al-Kasnazān, *Mawsū'ah al-Kasnazān fīmā Aṣṭalaḥa 'Alayhi Ahl al-Taṣawwuf wa al-'Irfān,* vol. 12, p. 39.

257 Ibid.

258 Al-Bukhārī, *Saḥīḥ Al-Bukhārī,* Hadith 6033; Muslim, *Ṣaḥīḥ Muslim,* Hadith 2307.

259 Ibn Kathīr, Qiṣaṣ al-Anbiyā', p. 451.

260 Ibid.

261 Al- Tādhafī, Qalā'id al-Jawāhir, p. 18; Ibn Mubarak, *Al-Ibrīz min Kalām Sīdī*

ʿAbd al-ʿAzīz al-Dabbāgh, p. 261.

262 Al-Sayyadī, *Tanwīr al-Abṣār fī Ṭabaqāt al-Sādah al-Rifāʿiyyah al-Akhyār*, p. 4.

263 Al-Safārīnī, *Al-Qawl al-ʿAlī li Sharḥ Athar al-Imām ʿAlī*, p. 73.

264 Al-Suyūṭī, *Tārīkh al-Khulafā'*, p. 151.

265 Ibid.

266 Al-Ṭūsī, *Akhlāq Nāṣirī*, p. 186

267 Ibn Kathīr, *Al-Bidāyah wa al-Nihāyah*, vol. 8, p. 169.

268 Al-Khawārizmī, *Maqtāl al-Ḥusayn*, p. 273.

269 Al-Ghamīdī, *Nuṣūṣ min Tārīkh Abī Mikhnaf*, vol. 1, p. 442.

270 Ibn Kathīr, *Al-Bidāyah wa al-Nihāyah*, vol. 8, p. 187.

271 Al-Jīlānī, *Al-Ghunyah*, p. 318.

272 Al-Shablanjī, *Nūr al-Abṣār*, p. 213.

273 Ibid, p. 217.

274 Al-Mu'ayyidī, *Al-Tuḥf Sharḥ al-Zalaf*, p. 52.

275 Al-Aṣbahānī, *Maqātil al-Ṭālibīn*, pp. 140141.

276 Al-Tamīmī, *Ghurār al-Ḥikam wa Durar al-Kalim*, p. 165.

277 Ibid.

278 Al-Kasnazān, *Mawsūʿah al-Kasnazān fīmā Aṣṭalaḥa ʿAlayhi Ahl al-Taṣawwuf wa al-ʿIrfān*, vol. 12, p. 40.

279 Ibid, p. 39.

280 Al-Kasnazān, *Mawsūʿah al-Kasnazān fīmā Aṣṭalaḥa ʿAlayhi Ahl al-Taṣawwuf wa al-ʿIrfān*, vol. 20, p. 128.

281 Al-Qāshānī, *Ādāb al-Ṭarīqah wa Asrār al-Ḥaqīqah fi Risa'il al-Sheikh Abd al-Razzaq al-Qāshānī*, p. 33.

282 Ibid.

283 Al-Tamīmī, *Ghurār al-Ḥikam wa Durar al-Kalim*, p. 357.

284 Muslim, *Ṣaḥīḥ Muslim*, Hadith 55.

285 Al-Qāshānī, *Ādāb al-Ṭarīqah wa Asrār al-Ḥaqīqah*, p. 33.

286 Ibid.

287 Al-Miʿmār, *Kitāb al-Futuwwah*, p. 72.

288 Muslim, *Ṣaḥīḥ Muslim*, Hadith 2592.

289 Al-Tamīmī, *Ghurār al-Ḥikam wa Durar al-Kalim*, p. 153.

290 Abū Dāwūd, *Sunan Abī Dāwūd*, Hadith 4918.

291 Al-Tamīmī, *Ghurār al-Ḥikam wa Durar al-Kalim*, p. 175.

292 Ibid.

293 Al-Bukhārī, *Saḥīḥ Al-Bukhārī*, Hadith 7376.

294 Al-Miʿmār, *Kitāb al-Futuwwah*, p. 204.

295 Dem, *Tafsīr Ḍiyā' al-Nayyirīn*, vol. 17, p. 118.

296 Al-Sulamī, *Adab al-Ṣuḥbah wa Ḥusn al-ʿIshrah*, p. 46.

297 Dem, *Tafsīr Ḍiyā' al-Nayyirīn*, vol. 17, p. 121.

298 Abduh, *Sharḥ Nahj al-Balāghah*, p. 484.

299 Al-Tamīmī, *Ghurār al-Ḥikam wa Durar al-Kalim*, p. 148.

300 Al-Bukhārī, *Sahib Al-Bukhārī*, Hadith 6065; Muslim, *Ṣaḥīḥ Muslim*, Hadith 2559.

301 Ibn Fūdī, *Mukhtārāt min Mu'allafāt li al-Shaykh ʿUthmān ibn Fūdī*, vol. 3, p. 51.

302 Al-Malībārī, *Al-Shaykh Muʿīn al-Dīn Jishtī al-Ajmirī*, p. 43.

303 Al-Bayhaqī, *Shuʿab al-Īmān*, Hadith #5137.

304 Al-Ṭabarānī, Al-Muʿjam al-Awsāṭ, Hadith #8210.

305 Ibn al-Athīr, Al-Mukhtār min Manāqib al-Akhyār, vol. 2, p. 449.

306 Ibn Kathīr, *Al-Bidāyah wa al-Nihāyah*, vol. 9, p. 115.

307 Ibn al-Jawzī, *Ṣifah al-Ṣafwah*, p. 357.

308 Al-Ṭabarī, *Tafsīr Al-Ṭabarī*, vol. 8, pp. 213-215.

309 Ibn al-Athīr, *Al-Mukhtār min Manāqib al-Akhyār*, vol. 3, p. 322.

310 Ibid, p. 328.

311 Al-Bukhārī, *Saḥīḥ Al-Bukhārī*, Hadith 6103.

312 Ibid, Hadith 6064.

313 Al-Kasnazān, *Mawsūʿah al-Kasnazān fīmā Aṣṭalaḥa ʿAlayhi Ahl al-Taṣawwuf wa al-ʿIrfān*, vol. 16, p. 35.

314 Al-Ṭūsī, *Akhlāq Nāṣirī*, p. 171.

315 Ibid.

316 Al-Kasnazān, *Mawsūʿah al-Kasnazān fīmā Aṣṭalaḥa ʿAlayhi Ahl al-Taṣawwuf wa al-ʿIrfān*, vol. 16, p. 35.

317 Al-Tamīmī, *Ghurār al-Ḥikam wa Durar al-Kalim*, p. 193.

318 Al-Ṭabarī, *Tafsīr Al-Ṭabarī*, vol. 6, p. 154.

319 Al-Zamakhsharī, *Tafsīr al-Kashshāf*, p. 944.

320 Ibid.

321 Ibn Ḥanbal, *Musnad Aḥmad*, Hadith 1584.

322 Riggeon, *Jawanmardi: A Sufi Code of Honour*, p. 49.

323 Al-Zamakhsharī, *Tafsīr al-Kashshāf*, p. 195.

324 Al-Bayhaqī, *Shuʿab al-Īmān*, Hadith 7964.

325 Al-Kasnazān, *Mawsūʿah al-Kasnazān*, vol. 4, p. 479.

326 Al-Bukhārī, *Al-Adab al-Mufrad*, Hadith 109.

327 Al-Bukhārī, *Saḥīḥ Al-Bukhārī*, Hadith 6015; Muslim, *Ṣaḥīḥ Muslim*, Hadith 2625.

328 Al-Bukhārī, *Al-Adab al-Mufrad,* Hadith 128.

329 Al-Nasa'ī, *Sunan Al-Nasa'ī,* Hadith 4995.

330 Al-Bukhārī, *Al-Adab al-Mufrad,* Hadith 118.

331 Al-Ṭabarānī, *Al-Mu'jam al-Awsāṭ,* Hadith 598.

332 Al-Tustarī, *Tafsīr al-Tustarī,* p. 150.

333 Al-Tirmidhī, *Sunan al-Tirmidhī,* Hadith 2317; Ibn Mājah, *Sunan Ibn Mājah,* Hadith 3976.

334 Ibid.

335 Muslim, *Ṣaḥīḥ Muslim,* Hadith 2625.

336 Ibn Ḥanbal, *Kitāb al-Zuhd,* Hadith 926.

337 Ibn al-Mi'mār, *Kitāb al-Futuwwah,* pp. 256-257.

338 Al-Tamīmī, *Ghurār al-Ḥikam wa Durar al-Kalim,* p. 180.

339 A provision for a guest that is superior to one's everyday meal.

340 Al-Bukhārī, *Al-Adab al-Mufrad,* Hadith 741.

341 Al-Ghazālī, *Mukāshafah al-Qulūb al-Muqarrab ilā 'Allām al-Ghuyūb,* p. 89.

342 'Afīfī, *Al-Malāmatiyyah wa al-Ṣufiyyah wa Ahl Futuwwah,* p. 47.

343 Al-Nasa'ī, *Sunan Al-Nasa'ī,* Hadith 5017.

344 Ibn Qayyim, *Madārij al-Sālikīn bayna Manāzīl Iyyāka Na'bud wa Iyyāka Nasta'īn,* p. 540.

345 Al-Mi'mār, *Kitāb al-Futuwwah,* pp. 262-263.

346 Al-Ḥākim, *Al-Mustadrak 'ala al-Ṣaḥiḥayn,* Hadith 2027.

347 Al-Tustarī, *Tafsīr al-Tustarī,* p. 165.

348 Al-Sulamī, *Tafsīr al-Sulamī,* vol. 2, p. 218.

349 Al-Yadālī, *Al-Dhahab al-Ibrīz fī Tafsīr Kitāb Allah al-'Azīz,* vol. 7, p. 93.

350 Al-Kalbī, *Al-Tashīl li al-'Ulūm al-Tanzīl,* vol. 2, p. 485.

351 Al-Mi'mār, *Kitāb al-Futuwwah,* pp. 261-262.

352 Ibn Qayyim, *Madārij al-Sālikīn bayna Manāzīl Iyyāka Na'bud wa Iyyāka Nasta'īn,* p. 539.

353 Ibid.

354 Al-Ardabīlī, *Futuwwah,* p. 10.

355 Ibn al-Mi'mār, *Kitāb al-Futuwwah,* p. 141.

356 Ibid, pp. 241 - 242

357 Ibn Qayyim, *Madārij al-Sālikīn bayna Manāzīl Iyyāka Na'bud wa Iyyāka Nasta'īn,* p. 540.

358 Ibn al-Mubarrid, *Irshād al-Salik ilā Manāqib Mālik,* p. 99.

359 Ibn Ḥanbal, *Musnad Aḥmad,* Hadith 27490.

NOTES

Bibliography

Publisher's Note: A few of the sources referenced in this book such as Akhlaq Nasiri, which is considered the first book written solely about the subject of Islamic ethics, are non-Sunni references. Though we are from the People of the Sunnah and the author is Sunni, the specific quotes taken from those sources, which were not frequently referenced, coincide with the traditional Sunni framework of al-Futuwwah, and do not conflict with the Qur'an and the authentic Prophetic sunnah. Thus, we believe that there was no harm in including these limited references.

PUBLISHED SOURCES

Al-ʿAbbāsī, Al-Nāṣir li Dīn Allah. *Kitāb Rūḥ al-ʿArifīn min Kalām Sayyid al-Mursalīn* (Amman: Dār al-Fikr, 2001).

ʿAbduh, M. *Sharḥ Nahj al-Balāghah* (Beirut: Mu'assasah bint al-Hudā, 2015).

Ibn Abī al-Ḥadīd, ʿAbd al-Ḥamīd. *Sharḥ Nahj al-Balāghah* (Beirut: Mu'assasah al-ʿAlā, 1995).

Ibn Abī Shaybah, Abū Bakr. *Al-Muṣannaf* (Riyadh, Maktabah al-Rushd, 2004).

ʿAfīfī, Abū al-ʿUlā. *Al-Malāmatiyyah wa al-Ṣufiyyah wa Ahl Futuwwah* (Beirut: Manshūrāt al-Jamāl, 2015).

Ibn Aḥmad, al-Qāsim. *Al-Ṭarā'if al-Mushtaqīn min Qiṣaṣ al-Awliyā' wa al-Ṣāliḥīn* (Sana'a: Mu'assasah al-Imam Zayd ibn ʿAlī al-Thaqāfiyyah, 2008).

Ibn ʿAlī, Zayd. *Tafsīr Gharīb al-Qur'ān al-Manṣūb ilā al-Imām Zayd ibn ʿAlī ibn al-Ḥusayn* (Beirut: Dār al-Waʿī al-Islāmī, 2015).

Al-ʿĀmilī, M. *Al-Kashkūl* (Beirut: Mu'assasah al-ʿĀlamī, 1999).

Amīn, A. *Al-Salʿakah wa al-Futuwwah fī al-Islām* (Cairo: Hindawi Foundation for Education and Culture, 2012).

Al-Anṣārī, 'Abdullāh. *Manāzil al-Sā'irīn* (Beirut: Manṣūrāt al-Riḍā', 2010).

Al-Ardabīlī, Aḥmad. *Futuwwah* (Amman: Dār al-Rāzī, 2002).

Al-Aṣbahānī, Abū al-Faraj. *Maqātil al-Ṭālibīn* (Beirut: Mu'assasah al-'Ālamī, 2007).

Al-Aṣbahānī, Abū Nu'aym. *Taḥdhīb Ḥilyah al-Awliyā' wa Ṭabaqāt al-Aṣfiyā'* (Beirut: Al-Maktabah al-Islāmī, 1998).

Al-Aṣbahānī, Al-Rāghib. *Muḥāḍarāt al-Udabā' wa Muḥāwarāt al-Shu'arā' wa al-Bulaghā'* (Beirut, Dār al-Arqam, 1999).

Ibn al-Athīr, Al-Mubārak. *Al-Mukhtār min Manāqib al-Akhyār* (Beirut: Dār al-Kutub al-'Ilmiyyah, 2009).

Azzam, A. *Saladin: The Triumph of the Sunni Revival,* 2nd New Edition (Cambridge: UK: The Islamic Texts Society, 2014).

Bamba, Aḥmadou. *Diwān al-'Ulūm al-Dīniyyah* (Rabat: Dār al-Aman, 2020).

Bā Sallūm, M. and Miskā, S. *Mawsū'ah Āl Bayt al-Nabī* (Beirut: Dār al-Kutub al-'Ilmiyyah , 2011).

Ibn Battuta, M. *The Travels of Ibn Battuta: In the Near East, Asia and Africa, 1325-1354,* trans. Samuel Lee (Dover Publications, 2013).

Al-Bayhaqī, Aḥmad. *Shu'ab al-Īmān* (Beirut: Dār al-Kutub, 2000).

Al-Bukhārī, Muhammad. *Al-Adab al-Mufrad* (Beirut: Dār al-Kutub al-'Ilmiyyah, 2019).

---. *Al-Jāmi' Al-Ṣaḥīḥ* (Riyadh: Dār ibn Hazm, 2015).

Al-Būṭī, Muhammad. *Fiqh al-Sunnah al-Nabawiyyah ma'a Mūjaz li Tārīkh al-Khilafah al-Rāshidah* (Damascus: Dār al-Fikr, 2019).

Al-Darqāwī, Muhammad. *Rasā'il Mawlay al-'Arab al-Darqāwī* (Beirut: Dār al-Kutub al-'Ilmiyyah, 2009).

Al-Daylamī, Abū Shujā', *Musnad al-Firdaws* (Beirut: Dār al-Kutub al-'Ilmiyyah, 2010).

Dem, Aḥmad. *Tafsīr Ḍiyā' al-Nayyirīn al-Jāmi' bayna 'Ulūm al-Tā'ifatayn* (Beirut: Dār al-Fikr, n.d.).

Al-Dhammarī, Yaḥyā. *Kitāb Taṣfīyah al-Qulūb* (Beirut: Mu'assasah al-Kutub al-Thaqāfiyyah, n.d.).

Al-Fayyūmī, Aḥmad. *Al-Miṣbāḥ al-Munīr fī Gharīb al-Sharḥ al-Kabīr* (Damascus: Al-Risālah al-'Ālamiyyah, 2015).

Fudi, ʿUthmān. *Mukhtārāt min Mu'allafāt li al-Shaykh ʿUthmān ibn Fūdī* (Gada-Biyu: Iqra' Publishing House, 2013).

Al-Ghamīdī, Lūṭ. *Nuṣūṣ min Tārīkh Abī Mikhnaf* (Beirut: Dār al-Maḥajjah al-Bayḍā', 1999).

Al-Ghazālī, Abū Ḥāmid. *Iḥyā' ʿUlūm al-Dīn* (Jeddah: Dār al-Minhāj, 2019).

---. *Mukāshafah al-Qulūb al-Muqarrab ilā ʿAllām al-Ghuyūb* (Beirut: Dār al-Maʿrifah, 1996).

Al-Ghumārī, Aḥmad. *ʿAlī ibn Abī Ṭālib Imām al-ʿĀrifīn* (Cairo: Maktabah al-Qāhirah, 2017).

Ibn al-Ḥajjāj, Muslim. *Al-Jāmiʿ Al-Ṣaḥīḥ* (Riyadh: Bayt al-Afkār al-Dawliyyah, 1998).

Al-Ḥākim, Muhammad. *Faḍā'il Fāṭimah al-Zahra* (Tehran: Al-Majmaʿ al-ʿĀlami li Ahl al-Bayt, 2012).

---. *Al-Mustadrak ʿala al-Ṣaḥiḥayn* (Beirut: Dār al-Kutub al-ʿIlmiyyah, 2011).

Ibn Ḥanbal, Aḥmad. *Kitāb al-Zuhd* (Beirut: Dār al-Kitāb al-ʿArabī, 2002).

---. *Musnad al-Imām Aḥmad ibn Ḥanbal* (Beirut: Mu'assasah al-Risālah, 2001).

Al-Ḥaskanī, ʿUbaydullāh. *Shawāhid al-Tanzīl li Qawāʿid al-Tafḍīl fī Ayāt al-Nāzilah fī Ahl al-Bayt* (Beirut: Mu'assasah al-'Ala, 1974).

Al-Haythamī, ʿAlī. *Majmūʿ al-Zawā'id wa Manbaʿ al-Fawā'id* (Beirut: Dār al-Kutub al-ʿIlmiyyah, 2001).

Ibn Ḥibbān, Abū Ḥātim. *Ṣaḥīḥ ibn Ḥibbān* (Beirut: Dār al-Kutub al-ʿIlmiyyah, 2014).

Al-Iskandarī, Ibn ʿAṭā' Allah. *Al-ʿAmāl al-Kāmilah* (Cairo: Dār al-Iḥsān, 2019).

ʿIṭr, M. *Al-Kāfī fī Fiqh al-Shāfiʿī* (Allepo: Dār al-Nahj li al-Dirāsāt wa al-Nashr wa al-Tawzīʿ 2007).

ʿIzzān, M. *Majmūʿ Kutub wa Rasā'il al-Imām Zayd ibn ʿAlī* (Sana'a: Dār al-Ḥikmah al-Yamaniyyah, 2001).

Ibn al-Jawzī, ʿAbd al-Raḥmān. *Dhamm al-Hawā* (Beirut: Dār al-Kutub al-ʿIlmiyyah, 2012).

---. *Manāqib al-Imām Aḥmad* (Cairo: Dar Ḥijr, 2008).

---. *Ṣifah al-Ṣafwah* (Beirut: Dār al-Kitāb al-ʿArabī, 2008).

Al-Jazarī, Shams al-Dīn. *Asmā' al-Manāqib fī Tahdhib Asnā al-Maṭālib fī Manāqib al-Imām Amīr al-Mu'minīn 'Alī ibn Abī Ṭālib* (Beirut: Dār al-Kutub al-'Ilmiyyah. 2005).

Al-Jīlānī, 'Abd al-Qādir. *Kitāb al-Bulbul al-Ṣādī bi Mawlid al-Hādī* (Istanbul: Markaz al-Jīlānī, 2014).

---. *Al-Fatḥ al-Rabbānī wa al-Fayḍ al-Rahmānī* (Beirut: Dār al-Kutub al-'Ilmiyyah, 2010).

---. *Kitāb al-Futuwwah fī Kayfiyyah Akhdh al-'Ahd wa al-Bay'ah* (Istanbul: Markaz al-Jīlānī, 2014).

---. *Al-Ghunyah li Tālib al-Tarīq al-Ḥaqq wa al-Dīn* (Beirut: Dār al-Khayr, 2005).

---. *Sirr al-Asrār wa Maẓhar al-Anwār fīmā Yaḥtāj ilayhi al-Abrār wa Yalīhi Futūḥ al-Ghayb wa Qalā'id al-Jawāhir fī Manāqib Tāj al-Awliyā' 'Abd al-Qādir wa Yalīhi Shams al-Fakhr wa Yalīhi al-Sayf al-Rabbānī fī 'Unuq al-Mu'tarid 'alā al-Ghawth al-Jilānī* (Beirut: Dār al-Kutub al-'Ilmiyyah, 2017).

---. *Tafsīr al-Jilānī* (Beirut: Dār al-Kutub al-'Ilmiyyah, 2014).

Al-Jurjānī, Al-Ḥusayn. *Al-I'tibār wa Salwah al-'Ārifīn* (Amman: Mu'assasah al-Imām Zayd ibn 'Alī al-Thaqāfiyyah, 2002).

Al-Kalbī, M. *Al-Tashīl li al-'Ulūm al-Tanzīl* (Beruit: Dar Iḥyā' al-Turāth al-'Arabī, 2004)

Al-Kasnazān, Muhammad. *Mawsū'ah al-Kasnazān fīmā Aṣṭalaha 'Alayhi Ahl al-Taṣawwuf wa al-'Irfān* (Beirut: Dar Verse, 2005).

Ibn Kathīr, Isma'īl. *Al-Bidāyah wa al-Nihāyah* (Beirut: Dār al-Kutub al-'Ilmiyyah, 2015).

---. *Al-Fuṣūl fī Sīrah al-Rasūl* (Riyadh: Maktabah al-Ma'ārif, 2000).

---. *Qiṣaṣ al-Anbiyā'* (Beirut: Dār al-Jīl, 2001).

Khachaturian, A. *Ahl al-Futuwwah wa al-Fityān fī al-Mujtamā' al-Islāmī* (Beirut: Markaz al-'Arabī li al-Abḥāth wa al-Tawthīq, 1998).

Al-Khaṭīb, As'ad. *Al-Buṭūlah wa al-Fidā 'Inda al-Ṣūfiyyah,* 5th ed. (Damascus: Dār al-Taqwā, n.d.).

Al-Khawārizmī, Al-Muwaffaq. *Muqtāl al-Ḥusayn* (Qom, Dār al-Anwār al-Hudā, 2010).

Al-Kubaysi, Aḥmad. *Mawsū'ah al-Kalimah wa Akhawātihā fī al-Qur'ān al-Karīm* (Beirut: Dār al-Ma'rifah, 2017).

Lukianoff, G. and Haidt, J. *The Coddling Of The American Mind: How Good Intentions And Bad Ideas Are Setting Up A Generation For Failure* (New York: Penguin Books, 2018).

Ibn Mājah, Muhammad. *Sunan Ibn Mājah* (Beirut: Dār al-Kutub al-ʿIlmiyyah, 2012).

Al-Malībārī, Muṣṭafā. *Al-Shaykh Muʿīn al-Dīn Jishtī al-Ajmīrī: Ḥayātuhu wa Daʿwatuhu wa Ātharuhu* (Beirut: Dār al-Kutub al-ʿIlmiyyah: 2018).

Ibn Manẓūr, Muhammad. *Lisān al-ʿArab* (Beirut: Mu'assasah al-ʿAlā, 2015).

Ibn al-Marzubān, Muhammad. *Kitāb Faḍl al-Kilāb min man Labisa al-Thiyāb* (Beirut: Manshūrāt al-Jamāl, 2016).

Ibn al-Miʿmār, Muhammad. *Kitāb al-Futuwwah* (Beirut: al-Warrāq, 2012).

Moore, R. and Gillette, D. *King Warrior Magician Lover: Rediscovering the Archetypes of the Mature Masculine, New edition* (San Francisco: Bravo Ltd, 1992).

Al-Mu'ayyidī, Majd al-Dīn. *Al-Tuḥf Sharḥ al-Zalaf* (Sana'a: Mu'assasah Ahl al-Bayt, 1993).

Ibn Mubārak, Aḥmad. *Al-Ibrīz min Kalām Sīdī ʿAbd al-ʿAzīz al-Dabbāgh* (Beirut: Dār Ṣādir, 2004).

Ibn al-Mubarrid, Yūsuf. *Irshād al-Sālik ilā Manāqib Mālik* (Beirut: Dar ibn Hazam, 2009).

Ibn Mufliḥ, Muhammad. *Al-Ādāb al-Sharʿiyyah wa al-Minaḥ al-Marʿiyyah* (Cairo: Dār al-Wafā', 2009).

Ibn Muhammad, Jaʿfar. *Miṣbāḥ al-Sharīʿah* (Beirut: Mu'assasah al-ʿĀlamī, 1992).

Murad, A. *Commentary on the Eleventh Contentions* (Cambridge: Quilliam Press, 2012).

---. *Travelling Home: Essays on Islam in Europe* (Cambridge: Quilliam Press Ltd, 2020).

Ibn Mūsā, ʿIyād. *Al-Shifā' bi Taʿrīf Huqūq al-Muṣṭafā* (Beirut: Dār al-Kutub al-ʿIlmiyyah, 2000).

Nadwi, A. *Prophet Of Mercy: Nabiyy-i Rahmat,* ed. Shoaib Shah et al., trans. Mohiuddin Aḥmad (London: Turath Publishing, 2020).

Al-Nawawī, Abū Zakariyyā. *Al-Minhāj fī Sharḥ Ṣaḥīḥ Muslim ibn al-Ḥajjāj* (Beirut: Mu'assasah al-Risālah, 2015).

Al-Nāqib, Aḥlām. *Siyāsah al-Khalīfah al-Nāṣir li Dīn Allah al-Dākhīliyyah* (Baghdad: Dār al-Shu'ūn al-Thaqāfiyyah al-ʿĀmah).

Al-Nasa'ī, Aḥmad. *Kitāb Khaṣā'iṣ Amīr al-Mu'minīn ʿAlī ibn Abī Ṭālib* (Beirut: Dār al-Kitāb al-ʿArabī, 1996).

---. *Sunan Al-Nasa'ī* (Beirut: Dār al-Maʿrifah, 2007).

Ibn al-Qayyim, Muhammad. *Al-Jawāb al-Kāfī* (Beirut: Dar Ibn Kathīr, 2016).

---. *Madārij al-Sālikīn bayna Manāzīl Iyyāka Naʿbud wa Iyyāka Nastaʿīn* (Beirut: Dār al-Kutub al-ʿIlmiyyah, 2010).

---. *Zād al-Maʿād* (Beirut: Mu'assasah al-Risālah, 2009).

Al-Quḍāʿī, Muhammad. *Musnad al-Shihāb* (Beirut: Dār al-Kutub al-ʿIlmiyyah, 2011).

Al-Qashānī, ʿAbd al-Razzāq. *Ādāb al-Ṭarīqah wa Asrār al-Ḥaqīqah* (Beirut: Dār al-Kutub al-ʿIlmiyyah, 2018).

Al-Qushayrī, ʿAbd al-Karīm. *Al-Risālah al-Qushayriyyah fī ʿIlm al-Taṣawwuf* (Beirut: Dār al-Kitāb al-ʿArabī, 2005).

Rabīʿah, Muṣṭafā. *Rasā'il al-Asmār ʿAbd al-Salām ibn Sālim al-Idrīsī Ḥasanī Marīdīh* (Benghazi, Dār al-Midār al-Islāmī, 2003).

Ridgeon, L. *Jawanmardi: A Sufi Code of Honour* (Edinburg: Edinburg University Press, 2011).

Ibn al-Ṣabbāgh, ʿAlī. *Al-Fuṣūl al-Muhimmah fī Maʿrifah Aḥwāl al-A'immah ʿAlayhim al-Salām* (Beirut: Mu'assasah Al-ʿAlā, 1988).

Al-Safārīnī, Muhammad. *Al-Qawl al-ʿAlī li Sharḥ Athar al-Imām ʿAlī Waṣiyyātuh h li Kumayl ibn Ziyād al-Nakhaʿī* (Beirut: Dār al-Bashā'ir al-Islāmīyyah, 2008).

Al-Sakhāwī, Muhammad. *Ṭabaqāt al-Awliyā' al-Mukarramīn* (Amman: Dār al-Fatḥ, 2020).

Al-Ṣanʿā'ī, ʿAbd al-Razzāq, *Tafsīr ʿAbd al-Razzāq* (Beirut: Dār al-Kutub al-ʿIlmiyyah, 1999).

Al-Sayyadī, Muhammad. *Bawāriq al-Ḥaqā'iq* (Beirut: Dār al-Kutub al-ʿIlmiyyah, 2011).

Sax, L. *Boys Adrift: The Five Factors Driving The Growing Epidemic Of Unmotivated Boys And Underachieving Young Men* (New York: Basic Books, 2009).

Al-Shaʿrānī, ʿAbd al-Wahhāb. *Al-Ṭabaqāt al-Kubrā* (Beirut: Dār al-Kutub al-ʿIlmiyyah, 2018).

Al-Shablanjī, Mu'min. *Nūr al-Abṣār fī Manāqib Āl Bayt al-Nabī al-Mukhṭār* (Beirut: Dār al-Kutub al-ʿIlmiyyah, 2008).

Al-Sijistānī, Abū Dāwūd. *Sunan Abī Dāwūd* (Damascus: Al-Risālah al-ʿĀlamiyyah, 2008).

Sukayrij, Aḥmad. *Kashf al-Ḥijāb ʿAmman Talaqā maʿa al-Shaykh al-Tijānī min al-Aṣḥāb* (Beirut: Al-Maktabah al- Shaʿbiyyah, n.d.).

Al-Suhrawardī, ʿUmar. *ʿAwārif al-Maʿārif* (Beirut: Dār al-Kutub al-ʿIlmiyyah, 2016).

Al-Sulamī, Muhammad. *Adab al-Ṣuḥbah wa Ḥusn al-ʿIshrah* (Beirut: Dār al-Warrāq, 2017).

---. *Futuwwah* (Amman: Dār al-Razi, 2001).

---. *Tafsir al-Sulamī* (Beirut: Dār al-Kutub al-ʿIlmiyyah, 2016).

Al-Ṣuyūṭī, Jalāl al-Dīn. *Sunan al-Nasa'ī bi Sharḥ al-Suyūṭī wa Ḥāshiyah al-Sanad* (Beirut: Dār al-Maʿrifah, 2008).

---. *Al-Jāmiʿ al-Ṣaghīr fī Aḥadīth al-Bashīr al-Nadhīr* (Beirut: Dār al-Kutub al-ʿIlmiyyah, 2008).

---. *Tārīkh al-Khulafā'* (Beirut: Dār al-Maʿrifah, 1997).

Al-Ṭabarānī, Sulayman. *Maqtal al-Ḥusayn ibn ʿAlī ibn Abī Ṭālib* (Kuwait City: Dār al-Awrād, 1992).

---. *Al-Muʿjam al-Awsāṭ* (Beirut: Dār al-Kutub al-ʿIlmiyyah, 1999).

---. *Al-Muʿjam al-Kabīr* (Mosul: Matbaʿah al-Zahra al-Ḥadīthah, 1984).

Al-Ṭabarī, Abū Jaʿfar. *Tafsīr al-Ṭabarī* (Beirut: Dār al-Kutub al-ʿIlmiyyah, 1992).

Al-Tamīmī, ʿAbd al-Wāḥid. *Ghurār al-Ḥikam wa Durar al-Kalim* (Beirut: Mu'assasah al-ʿAlami, 2002).

Al-Thāmīrī, Iḥsān, and al-Qadḥāt, Muhammad. *Rasā'il min al-Turāth al-Ṣūfī fī Labs al-Khirqah* (Amman: Dār al-Razi, 2002).

Al-Tirmidhī, Abū ʿĪsā. *Al-Shamā'il al-Muḥammadiyyah wa al-Khaṣā'il al-Muṣṭafawiyyah* (Beirut: Dār al-Kutub al-ʿIlmiyyah, 1996).

---. *Sunan al-Tirmidhī* (Beirut: Dār al-Kutub al-ʿIlmiyyah, 2017).

Al-Ṭūsī, Nāṣir al-Dīn. *Akhlāq Nāṣirī* (Beirut: Dar al-Hādī, 2008).

Al-Wāsiṭī, Sharaf al-Dīn. *Al-Burhān al-Mu'ayyid li Ṣāḥib Madd al-Yad Mawlāna al-Ghawth al-Sharīf al-Rifāʿī Aḥmad* (Beirut: Dār al-Kutub al-ʿIlmiyyah, 2010).

Al-Yadālī, Muhammad. *al-Dhahab al-Ibrīz fī Tafsīr Kitāb Allah al-ʿAzīz* (Casablanca: Manshūrāt Markaz Najibawiyyah, 2014).

Al-Zamakhsharī, Maḥmūd. *Asās al-Balāghah* (Beirut: Dār al-Kutub al-ʿIlmiyyah, 2010).

———. *Tafsīr al-Kashshāf* (Beirut: Dār al-Maʿrifah, 2005).

Zimbardo, P. *Man Disconnected: How the Digital Age Is Changing Young Men Forever* (London: Rider, 2016).

Al-Zuʿbī, ʿAbd al-Majīd. *Itḥāf al-Akābir fī Sīrah wa Manāqib al-Imām Muḥyī al-Dīn ʿAbd al-Qādir al-Jīlanī al-Ḥasanī al-Ḥusaynī* (Beirut: Dār al-Kutub al-ʿIlmiyyah, 2007).

UNPUBLISHED SOURCES

Fall, S. *Al-Khidmah* ʿInda *al-Shaykh al-Khādim Bayna al-Naẓariyyah wa al-Tatbīq* (Dakkar: Cheikh Anta Diop University, 2008).

Al-Sayyadī. *Tanwīr al-Abṣār fī Ṭabaqāt al-Sādah al-Rifāʿiyyah al-Akhyār* (Misr: Matbaʿāt Muhammad Afandi Muṣṭafā, 1889).

www.ingramcontent.com/pod-product-compliance
Lightning Source LLC
Chambersburg PA
CBHW022119160426
43197CB00009B/1085
* 9 7 8 1 9 5 2 3 0 6 3 9 6 *